ABUSE
of Christian Women in India

Jane A. McNally

and

REMEDY
in 12 Biblical Studies
on Equality of Man and Woman

Berkeley and Alvera Mickelsen

ABUSE
of Christian Women in India

Jane A. McNally

and

REMEDY
in 12 Biblical Studies
on Equality of Man and Woman

Berkeley and Alvera Mickelsen

Pasadena, California
www.WCLBooks.com

Abuse of Christian Women in India & Remedy in 12 Biblical Studies on Equality of Man and Woman
Copyright © 2005 by Jane A. McNally

All rights reserved.
No part of this work may be reproduced or transmitted in any form or by any means—for example, electronic or mechanical, including photocopying and recording—without prior written permission of the publisher.

Scripture taken from the HOLY BIBLE, NEW INTERNATIONAL VERSION. Copyright © 1973, 1978, 1984 International Bible Society. Used by permission of Zondervan Bible Publishers.

Cover design: Chris Kim

Published by William Carey Library
1605 E. Elizabeth Street
Pasadena, California 91104
www.WCLbooks.com

William Carey Library is a Ministry of the U.S. Center for World Mission, Pasadena, California.

ISBN 0-87808-347-2

Printed in the United States of America

This book was originally published by ISPCK in Delhi, India, in 1997 and 1999 (ISBN 81-7214-348-6).

Contents

Foreword vii

Part I: Abuse of Christian Women in India 1
Preface to Part I 3
Abuse of Christian Women in India 5

Part II: Remedy in 12 Biblical Studies 23
Preface to Part II 25
Lesson 1: Backgrounds for Sexual Discrimination 27
Lesson 2: How Do We Interpret the Bible 30
Lesson 3: God's Ideal and How It was Destroyed by Sin 36
Lesson 4: Men and Women in the Old Testament 39
Lesson 5: Jesus' Attitude Toward Women and Men 42
Lesson 6: Women and Men in the Early Church 45
Lesson 7: Husbands and Wives in Marriage 48
Lesson 8: The Meaning of "Head" in the New Testament 51
Lesson 9: Regulations for People in Corinth 58
Lesson 10: Regulations for People in Ephesus 62
Lesson 11: Teaching about Authority in the Bible 66
Lesson 12: The Gifts God Gives to Believers 69
Appendix 71

Foreword

Abuse of women, which takes many forms through the creativity of clever and mighty men, seems accepted in many cultures. The issue does not seem to bother society to any significant degree. Some societies, as though wanting to outdo others, seem to major in female abuse. With pain I acknowledge that my own contemporary Indian society is one such. What is more hurting and shameful is that women are abused in Indian Christian homes. The Christian home and abuse of women? Yes, the terms are contradictory, but a reality in contemporary India. Abuse is an issue that conscientious Christians need to address urgently, in order to arrest this dehumanizing, shameful, even cruel practice, so that the name of Jesus Christ may not continue to be dishonoured, that women created in God's image may enjoy their God-given dignity and worth. So that Christian homes may be what they are meant to be.

In this setting, this little book on the abuse of Christian women in India and the remedy, which lies in understanding and promoting the true biblical and God-given relationship of woman and man, deserves our careful attention. Ms. Jane McNally, who spent most of her life in India, bares the tip of the problem of abuse in Indian Christians' homes with accuracy and authority, also with pain and passion. The solution is in the Word of God, and Dr. Berkeley and Alvera Mickelsen's Bible study outlines are of tremendous help in this regard. We need to understand and submit to the Bible's authority and standard, to redeem our family life.

I sincerely hope that Ms. McNally's candid presentation of the reality in many of our homes will awaken our sensitivity and shame, and the Mickelsens' Bible studies will enable us to understand the Biblical standard clearly and perceptively and bring our lives in line with God's standard. I commend the authors for their passion and concern for Christian homes, and am happy to recommend this book to the Christian community in India and to anyone who would like to know and profit by what the Word of God says about women and family and church life. I pray that this little book will contribute to an attitudinal change and transformation in all of us, so that homes where Christ's lordship is demonstrated will be a significant witness to society at large. I trust that theological colleges and seminaries in our land would find this book helpful in the training of Christian leadership in our churches.

Rev. Dr. C. V. Mathew
Chennai

Part 1

ABUSE
of Christian Women in India

Jane A. McNally

Preface

The first edition told with some detail how this book came to be written. In brief, I was asked to prepare a paper for a coming consultation in Chicago on "Women, Abuse, and the Bible," being arranged by an organization that seeks, through Bible exposition and testimony, to promote equality in dignity and worth of all people without regard to gender, race, age, or class. Learning that I had served for long years in India and had some knowledge of the abuse problem there, the chairman asked me to present a paper on abuse of Christian women in India.

I consented, because the subject is of considerable concern to me. I began with no files or gathered materials, just a few memories. But a fairly wide acquaintance and friends gained in India over the years could provide information. Their contributions, added to my knowledge and experience, resulted in the paper which I presented to one of 28 seminars in the consultation held in 1994, attended by 150 invited social workers, family counsellors, teachers, and pastors. The paper was well received.

At the time I did not think beyond its possible benefit to some of the many thousands from India studying or resident in the USA. But the desire grew of making it of help to the Christian community in India.

The sponsoring organization for the consultation, Christians for Biblical Equality, had a display of their books during the sessions. I had bought a small book by the late Professor A. Berkeley Mickelsen and his wife, Alvera, consisting mainly of expanded Bible study outlines on the equality of man and woman.

As I read it, I saw that the booklet gave clear understanding of God's purpose in both creation and redemption for the lives and relationships of humankind. My paper would give a wake-up call needed by society, church, and family concerning the inferior position of the vast majority even of Christian women in India; and the Mickelsens' text could give biblical insights for healing the wrongs being done to them. Alvera freely gave consent to team my paper with the Bible studies, slightly re-edited, for readers of English in India.

Professor C. V. Mathew and his family were in the USA at the time. Reading the paper, the teenaged daughter told her father that it must be published in India. Dr. Mathew agreed with the Mickelsens' studies also, but suggested questions that critics would raise. This led to the addition of an appendix, which has now been expanded in this edition. So the book in two parts came to be, when ISPCK, with no hesitation, agreed to publish it. The lack of teaching in Christian institutions and churches needed to bring healing had become increasingly evident as I came to see the extent of the abuse and the persons affected. The first edition has already brought a change of attitude to at least some. Most of Part Two has been drawn from the writings of highly qualified and insightful Christian men. Men perhaps need this teaching most, for it is they whose change in understanding and behaviour can lift the spirits and give new direction to women, who for long centuries have had a sense of inferiority and subservience instilled in them from earliest childhood. It is my prayer that there will be help to other communities also, as they see an increase in truly Christian gender relationships.

Thanks are due to Tyndale House Foundation for the generous subsidy to keep the price affordable for students and womens groups. Heartfelt thanks also to Alvera Mickelsen, whose generous help and cooperative spirit have added greatly to this venture.

Jane McNally
Newberg, Oregon

ABUSE OF CHRISTIAN WOMEN IN INDIA

by Jane McNally

The second class status and sad plight of a majority of India's women is general knowledge and distresses no one more than thinking Indian citizens themselves. Despite the vast potential of its people and natural resources of the country, India is near the bottom in world rankings as regards quality of life of women and girls.[1]

The 1901 national census had shown a ratio of 972 women to 1000 men. This ratio had dropped steadily and alarmingly to a figure of 929 women to 1000 men in 1991, despite the rise in life expectancy to a fairly respectable 58 years for the general populace. There had been a brief upturn in numbers of women by percentage in 1981, then down again with the advent of gender selection in abortion by amniocentesis.[2]

In the general public, women do not have individual identity and worth. They live in relation to the husband, to serve the husband. To the orthodox Hindu woman, her husband is her god. Stigma attaches to the unmarried and the widowed, and to parents who keep an unmarried daughter at home. Daughters may be loved, but the need of getting them married is a heavy, sometimes crippling burden, and sons are favoured and highly valued. Patriarchy and male domination are deeply entrenched. Fear of poverty and love of status feature also. This brief preamble gives background and perspective to the subject of abuse of Christian women in India.

One Small Community

My learning in this subject came early in my second term of missionary service. I had been given the charge of a newly developed outreach with Bible courses with postal tuition. A gifted missionary had crafted questions that would make the reader of a Gospel portion read and reread, searching out answers. Missionaries checked the English lesson papers, and a young Indian national was checking the Bible lessons in our state language, Marathi.

The senior missionary couple in charge were going on home leave and were pleased to have hired the son of a pastor in a neighbouring mission, and his new bride. Dipak had high school and two years of Bible school training. His young wife, Kiran, was one of our mission orphans raised in our girls' school and with two years of high school. A room with kitchen was rented for them from a Christian landlord.

The young couple, after instruction, were quietly tending to their work with the Marathi Bible lessons. Late one night Kiran came in the dark, in a state of desperation, asking for protection from her husband. Immediately I took her in, fastened the door, had her sit down, and listened to her story. Dipak was beating her every night, mercilessly, and that night he had started choking her. "If only he wouldn't beat me on the head," Kiran moaned. "Anywhere but on my head!"

I put her to bed, and for days that seemed the only place she wanted to be. Her young husband prowled around the bungalow at night, moaning, calling, beating on the window screens. He knew his work with us was terminated.

I had questioned the landlord who lived in the flat next to the young couple's. "He's love crazy," said the old gentleman. He keeps it up night after night and won't listen to reason. They need an older person living with them."

After a few days I let Dipak in to talk with Kiran, remaining in the room with them. He fell on his knees beside her bed, stroking her beaten legs and pleading with her in low tones. The next day he left. I had written to the missionary who served as Kiran's guardian and who was away in the hills on annual leave, and was waiting to hear where there would be a safe place to send the young woman.

In about a month Dipak was back and persuaded Kiran to leave with him. She was a young adult, so I had no choice but to let her go.

Later word came that Kiran was in advanced pregnancy. Dipak had pushed her up against the wall of their room, fiercely threatening her, with one hand gripping her throat to hold her fast, and with the other was holding a knife with its sharp point jabbed against her now distended abdomen.

Kiran was helped to get a divorce, then was sent to teacher training so she could support herself and the baby daughter born to her. She had her emotional ups and downs, but grew to be a helpful and compassionate woman.

Not long after the divorce Dipak married again. Later we heard that the second young wife had died and that Dipak had been put in jail. Then we lost track of him. Years later I learned that he was married and working in another state.

When the Christian landlord and I were recalling dear Kiran's case, I asked, with a smile, if he had ever hit his wife. Sheepishly, he said he had, in the early years. I turned to a young man who was standing nearby. He too, embarrassed, said he had done the same. No comment was needed.

A former missionary colleague has reminded me that a well liked and respected national pastor at this same mission station had struck his wife, a nurse of about his own age whom he had married after the death of his first wife. The incident occurred during the one time visit of a grown daughter by the first marriage. There had been some unpleasantness between the two women, and the father must have felt that the occasion called for showing favour to his daughter.

During my years in this up-country mission station I became aware of three more cases. In one, the pastor, a different one now, repeatedly was peacemaker and counsellor to a quarrelling couple. At least once the wife came for shelter in the middle of a cold winter's night, having been put out of the house as the culmination of a violent exchange. The pastor and his wife got up, dressed, took her home, and persuaded the fuming husband to let her in. With the years, the couple has mellowed.

In another of the cases the young husband, Arul, was a Hindu convert with a few years of Bible school training before he was sent for a full seminary course. Apparently no discipling or mentoring was done. When he came to our mission and soon married he was assigned to an area where he would be working without a companion and with little accountability. When the frequent beating and shouting was discovered and confronted, although Arul was not dismissed, he found mission work elsewhere.

Later he opted for secular work. The couple seem to have learned to accommodate to one another. Among other things, he may feel that secular work is where he belongs. The couple attend church regularly. (Names in all the foregoing have been altered.)

As this number of cases came to mind it surprised me, because the small Christian congregation was a peaceable one, always happy for social times that brought all of them together. There was sound preaching, and regular listening to Hindi and Marathi Christian radio broadcasts. But biblical exposition that could counter the prevailing male dominance of the national culture was never heard, because it was not taught in the Bible training schools and seminaries. It is worth noting that the six men mentioned here anonymously are from five different missions or churches, and from four different Christian training institutions. Most of them, with the exception of Dipak, were well-intentioned men who, I believe, would have responded to the teaching of gender equality and mutuality that we are hearing more of nowadays.

The churches of India are not equipped for surveying their membership in order to know the degree of abuse in the home. I have gained additional input from a few leading pastors in India and from retirees like me,[3] so I can say, regretfully, that there is far more abuse than one would expect among even nominal Christians. Yet, Christianity has made a marked difference, as we shall see later.

Others Heard From

A missionary surgeon recently retired from thirty-nine years at a mission hospital in South India has shared with me. She writes: "As to beating of wives in Christian homes, I don't have material. But I remember one of our nursing tutors telling me, when I noticed some bruises on her, 'Oh, my husband hit me. It just shows that he loves me. If he didn't beat me once in a while that would mean that he didn't care about me.' And she was quite proud of this. Other nurses standing around, also married, agreed that this was true. Certainly there is nothing said from the pulpit about it, and I suspect that even Christian wives accept it as normal."

Bill, a missionary principal for many years of a Bible College in Calcutta, wrote that he had nothing to contribute on wife abuse, only a retort of a villager. "If I don't beat my wife, how will she learn anything?"

Another friend, Donna, who was a missionary wife teaching in a seminary in northern India, tells of a student "who beat his wife and broke her arm and should have been expelled, but we were too lenient. Later, in another city, he became mentally deranged and was incarcerated for a time. The wife fled with the children to a Christian rehabilitation center for women and children. But that is atypical. The usual abuse among Christians is psychological, verbal, and demeaning."

She goes onto say, "Certainly wives are servants and are given a lesser place. They get little Christian teaching. Even if they get to church once a week they have all the care of babies and children, and may be out of the service more than in. When I had weekly classes for wives of seminary students, it was very difficult to persuade the men to let the women study for even one hour a week, while I tried to have the men take care of the children that hour. Men could sit in class, chapel, prayer meetings hours on end, for days, weeks, and years, yet think that wives needed no teaching! I tried to tell them that wives in India are not only perpetrators of religion and culture, but also trainers of the next generation. Lack of teaching for women is one reason for the horrendous amount of nominalism among second or third generation Christians around the world. Unless children are taught, as was Timothy, to apply scriptural truth to every attitude and practice, they will grow up pagans."

"About the tribals of northeast India," she continued, "the tribal women are already more free than others, and Christianity takes them further. One of our tribal women had been ordained a lay preacher in the Mizo Presbyterian Church; but some of our western faculty opposed training women at all! Indian men were far more open to the need for trained women to reach and teach the three-fourths of India comprised of women and children. Of course, even tribal Christian women do the lion's share of housework and child rearing. One tribal faculty man in our seminary would not even keep his son for two hours, on a free Saturday, so his wife could take a TEE test!"

Donna went on to say that their daughter, a missionary surgeon in Bangladesh, says that in that country men, even Christians, are expected to beat their wives to keep them under control. She has done considerable teaching of individuals against the practice. Donna's daughter gets very discouraged about the situation for women in Bangladesh, for pitiful cases of battered women are brought into the hospital. She says, "The worst thing in the world is to be a Bangladeshi woman!"

In an advanced Indian city an accomplished young Christian woman gave up hope for an abusive marriage to which she had tried to give her best for eight long years. Painfully, she decided on divorce. Her health was failing through physical, psychological, and sexual abuse, and the situation was affecting her young children also. She knew that misunderstanding and ostracism in the churches faced her. But her deeply grieving parents decided to stand with her in this crisis, as all attempts to redeem the marriage had failed. In the initial period of judicial separation from her husband (a Christian man with two graduate degrees), the young woman was able to encourage quite a number of other hurting Christian women who came to know of her circumstances because she was fairly prominent. She found shelter for a few and directed some to legal help. Much of this suffering might not have been if abuse in the home had been addressed from the pulpits of the city.

A missionary couple lived in an apartment building that had well educated Christian occupants, and told how, late one night, the young wife of a leading church officer came running down the hall and asked to be taken in because her husband was beating her. This man was highly trained for his profession, and the wife was college-educated.

Of course women as well as men need biblical teaching for recognizing the God-given equality and worth of women. The verbal and psychological abuse of daughters-in-law by mothers-in-law is proverbial in the culture. This too is the experience of some Christian women. Friends tell of a Christian home where the mother so continually and hurtfully abused her daughter-in-law that the son took his young wife and left, in anger. For shelter the couple had to throw themselves on the mercy of friends until the young husband could get a job in another city.

But I love to tell the story of Suvartabai, the beloved Bible-trained wife of a pastor whose daughter-in-law wept the most of any at her mother-in-law's funeral. The young wife said, "She never gave me an unkind word." Suvartabai was one among others who personify the Bible's Naomi.

A young man who was a popular and effective leader of Christian youth became the head of a new para church ministry funded from overseas. One day it was reported that he had slapped his wife in front of the staff. A courageous young woman went to see him about it and he confessed that the report was true, and said he would not do it again.

I believe that all of the persons mentioned thus far have some years of mission school education, and numbers of them have higher education in Christian institutions also. This is likely true in the cases that follow.

A senior pastor with wide experience says he had been "in evangelical oblivion" until a direct remark caused him to consider closely the marriages of some church workers and Christian leaders. He became greatly disturbed and disheartened to find evidence of wife beating in the homes of evangelicals, including those of leaders in the Christian community. The wives, on the whole, remained silent on the subject. One seminary graduate, employed in the seminary, whenever he chose would thrash his wife, who also was a seminary graduate. I since have learned that this abusive husband has reformed, through the counsel and prayers of colleagues.

Our senior pastor friend asked a minister of his own denomination what he knew about Christian workers beating their wives. The minister told him that it was "a general factor of experiential evidence. Even various pastors are doing it. As an ordained minister, I know it is so." The above-mentioned senior pastor continues: "A mainline minister, graduate of Madras Christian College and of an evangelical seminary, was beating his wife and terrorizing her and their son for years. This pastor feigned to be most spiritual, even strongly ascetic. The pathos of it is that the woman had been the first Indian lady staff worker in a Christian youth organization, with a postgraduate degree in literature. This man and wife left India several years ago for the USA, where he pastors a church."

I regret the telling, and so will you. It reads like a companion to the Alsdurfs' book.[4]

A few years ago I was visiting with a Christian leader who had come to the United States for ministry and to visit relatives and friends. One particular case of abuse in a Christian community in India came into the conversation. The host said flatly of certain individuals that they "beat up their wives." The only reason I share these things, and my friends have shared with me, is that open knowledge of the situation could lead to change. Change there must be.

That the male dominance and patriarchy of the Indian culture has influence on the Christian community is clearly evident from the foregoing. We can just as surely say, the effects of the Fall are evident. But Christianity nevertheless has made a great difference.

The Church and Dowry

Among the many letters received from our postal Bible students were some, like that of a young man from the South who wrote: "What can I do for my sister? Because of our poverty she will have to go into a convent. We have no dowry for her." I wonder about Patricia, described in a paper in Punjab as "a very pretty Christian girl who is absolutely terrified of her older husband who has been regularly beating her and resorting to sexual violence," including sodomy. How did she get into such a marriage? Could her parents not provide dowry for a better match? Patricia has found the courage to file a court case.[5]

From the brief account of the death of Darese John, may we conclude that it was a bride burning? It reads, "Because the crime takes place at home, evidence can be cleared away long before the police arrive. In the home of hostile in laws, there aren't any witnesses. When Darese John burned to death in 1984, none of the 25 in laws living in the same New Delhi house came to her rescue."

Dowry is a practice mainly of high caste Hindus in the North, but is spreading into the middle classes. The giving of dowry is common also among Syrian Christians in the South. Numbers move elsewhere in India for employment, taking the practice of dowry with them. The giving of dowry shifts the responsibility for the daughter to the marital family, and is meant to take the place of the inheritance she does not receive. Dowry has not been a constant practice in Indian history, but has been growing strongly in recent years, because of an enormously growing consumerism and desire for conveniences and possessions. Arid there is the status of being able to say, "We gave so much ...." Unscrupulous people have turned marriage into profit making, and the much publicised dowry deaths are a result.

Pastor Chandy, in northern India, for eighteen years did not have occasion to preach about the dowry system because it had never been a problem in his congregation. But then the problem presented itself. The daughter of a Christian mother and a Hindu father, the young woman herself with leanings toward Christianity and attending church with her mother, became a victim of dowry. She and a Christian youth, son of a recognized evangelical leader in another church, had been corresponding for four years. Every time the girl's parents contacted the boy's parents to negotiate a wedding date, they received some excuse for delay. Finally when there was delay again, the girl's mother asked, "Is there anything we need to do to speed up matters?"

She wished to learn whether the boy's parents were angling for dowry, which a friend suggested could be happening.

The boy's father said, "Well, our son is in the U.S., and we don't have a house of our own. He is not able to help us much, and after marriage he would be less able. If we had our own house we could easily go ahead with the marriage."[6]

"The Hindu father," wrote Pastor Chandy, "then dropped, the matter and married off his daughter to a. Hindu naval officer, an award holder for bravery. That family didn't ask for dowry and said, 'We only want a daughter.' But demands started after the marriage. The naval officer used his training to abuse and batter his bride in such a way that she would not be marked. She managed to escape, running away in her bathroom slippers, and a report was lodged at the police station the same day. "When we saw her she was curled up in bed like a hurt child, said Pastor Chandy. "On seeing us she just wept, and clung to my wife. Though over twenty-five she seemed like a fifteen year old, was always sorrowing, and asking, why."

Pastor Chandy is helping with her case. A young woman abused by a Hindu spouse. But Christians had played with her life and her future, over dowry.

This unhappy young woman tells of other dowry victims. One is a Christian girl whose parents arranged her marriage with a well-to-do-boy of the same community. Under pressure from the mother-in-law the girl was tortured for dowry and would have been burned to death, she reports, if she had not providentially escaped. A case has been registered by the police under the Anti Dowry Act.

Pastor Chandy now has written against the dowry system where it is entrenched in churches, in his ancestral Kerala. Dowry deaths are rare among Christians. But Chandy cogently says that by going along with the system, actually benefitting from it, the Syrian Christian Churches are silently abetting this enormous evil that is growing in the land. Dowry has been illegal since 1961, so the churches do not use the term itself. "Go betweens talk of dowry specifically, calling it *stree dhanam* (bride's wealth)," says Chandy. "Once initial negotiations are over the Kerala families may speak of dowry, but talk mostly of 'pocket money.' The pocket money may be from one lakh of rupees to five lakhs, depending on the 'price' of the groom, determined by his profession and earning power. At the time of engagement the priest asks, 'Is there any "giving" or "taking"?' The answer given may not be the truth. The priest then says, 'Just give the church whatever ought to be given to the church.'" The amount, it seems, is expected to be five percent of the stree *dhanan.*

I am told by another Keralite who opposes the dowry system that the *stree dhanam* is usually placed initially in a fixed deposit in the bride's name. The groom's family rationalizes that as they have to give for a daughter's marriage they have the right to ask at the time of a son's marriage. It is a vicious circle.

"In Kerala the dowry amount is settled before marriage," says Chandy. "There are no demands or bride burnings after marriage, except rarely. This new development could increase, taking the cue from the North."[7] Both illiteracy and Hindu fundamentalism are highest in northern India, and the effects of discrimination against women are strongest there. Daughters are considered an economic burden.

Happily, many Christians of Kerala stand against the dowry system and trust God for the right marriage for themselves, and for their children.

Right thinking non-Christian who deplore the demeaning and vulnerable position of Indian women, going at it from their stand point, see that economic independence and empowerment of women through education and gainful employment, and especially, equal inheritance rights, would give women a status and respect in the marital family that is now lacking. Economic empowerment would enable women if necessary to walk away from an abusive marriage. Male family members too would benefit, free of the dowry burden and the necessity of intervening when a daughter or sister is harassed! College students pledge to marry without dowry, but many lose that resolve when the time for marriage comes.

Mary Roy Fights Unjust Inheritance Law

John Clark Marshman, son of William Carey's colleagues Joshua band Hannah Marshman, worked with his parents in India, and published a series of law books including the *Guide to the Civil Law.*[9] For years the *Guide* was the civil code of India, and is background for The Indian Succession Act of 1925.

This Succession Act gives law relating to inheritance from Britishers domiciled in India or from Indian Christians who die intestate, without leaving a valid will. The Act gives a widow one-third and both son and daughter, or if deceased their children, or grandchildren, equal shares of the two-thirds of the property. [10] The Act did not, however, reach all of India's Christians, because two codes of law were in effect for the Syrian Christians of Travancore and Cochin, and the Syrian Church hierarchy resisted change in inheritance law. In 1951 the princely states of Travencore and Cochin had joined the Indian Union, becoming the state of Kerala. Technically, the Indian Succession Act should have applied to them then. The Travencore Christian Succession Act (1916) gave widows one third of the property for maintenance until death or remarriage, and daughters one-fourth the sons' share. The Cochin Christian Succession Act (1921) gave one-third to the widow, with complete right over it, and one-third the sons' share to daughters. In both bills the amount for daughters is limited to Rs 5,000, or whichever is less. This figure has not changed over the many intervening years. Mary Roy, a Christian woman of Travancore, contested the Travencore law and was joined by a widow with her six daughters, who had legally been put out of the family home by the one son. Women's organizations backed them. Mary Roy would have received her portion after her father's death, and no more when her mother died. Her brother has the total remaining inheritance.[11]

In 1986 the Supreme Court issued the verdict: "Mary Roy is eligible to the legal support of the 1924 Indian Succession Act like any other Indian Christian Woman from 1951 onwards." This was a great and historic victory for Christian women of Kerala. If the principle of equality in the verdict could spread to other communities, it would give status and economic means that could gain for women a respected place in their marital homes, where uncounted numbers now are servants to mothers-in-law and sisters-in-law and vulnerable to abuse for additional dowry.

But the victory of the Mary Roy case is not finalized, because politicians and church heads are lobbying vigorously for legislation to cancel the retrospective aspect of the Supreme Court Verdict. The Act would then have effect only from 1986, the year the verdict was made. Mary Roy and many others then would not benefit.

Women had not been silent before Mary made her case. There had been earlier cases asking for the equitable law. The first Law Minister for Kerala had introduced a one-sentence bill: "The Travencore Christian Succession Act and the Cochin Christian Succession Act stand null and void." But the bill was received coldly and was allowed to lapse. Christian men, supported by the Church, opposed changing the inheritance law then, and are now strongly opposing implementation of the law from 1951, the year Kerala joined the Union of States. [12]

In the various systems of Hindu law women had certain inalienable rights in ancestral property. The Hindu Succession Act of 1956 sought, for uniformity, to codify the various Hindu inheritance laws. As a consequence women lost some inheritance rights that had been favourable to them, and rights the Act did give them were not protected. With the new right for men to make wills, daughters could be, and often are, disinherited in favour of sons or nephews.[13]

The Koran safeguards inheritance rights for women, but a son gets double the daughter's share) [14]

Section 51 A(e) of the Indian Constitution says it is the fundamental duty of every citizen "to renounce practices derogatory to women." [15]

There is a long way to go, for India's women.

Marriage and Divorce

In 1978 the legal marriage age for all communities was increased, by the Sharda Act for Restraint of Child Marriage, to 21 years for men and 18 years for women. This is up from the 16 and 14 years that were declared legal in 1929.

In rural areas the new law is frequently bypassed, but extremely young brides live with their parents until puberty. The marrying of young girls to older men has resulted in a large population of widows in the Hindu community, many of whom live in dire poverty and beggary. Most Christians observe the legal age for marriage, although in rural areas some weddings continue to take place with the couple a few years younger.

The Indian Christian Marriage Act of 1872, still in effect, is based on English law. A minor can wed only with "an order of a Competent Court."[16] Among Christians the husband can sue for divorce for proven adultery. The wife can sue on the grounds of adultery, cruelty, marital rape or sodomy, and desertion. (This of course tells us that spousal abuse has long been in the western world. But there have been compassionate, fair-minded legislators who got protective legislation in place for women.) Alimony is set by the judge, according to circumstances. Annulment of a marriage, rendering it null and void, can be declared under Section IV,

19 of the Indian Divorce Act, 1869, if the respondent was impotent, if the parties were within the natural or legal prohibited degrees of blood relationship, if either was lunatic or idiot at the time of marriage, or if one of the parties had been previously married and the earlier marriage was still in force.[17]

In civil courts, divorce or annulment permits remarriage. The Catholic Church however does not sanction divorce, and so will annul a marriage that seems irretrievably broken. Some Protestant assemblies in India also do not sanction remarriage after divorce, and some individuals also take this position.

Tribal Christians come under the same Marriage Act, but aspects of their tribal law continue culturally. Among the Mizos of the Northeast, the vast majority of whom are Christian, there is no dowry. The groom gives a bride price, and gifts to the family members, in token, traditionally, for their loss of her labour. The bride price is also a statement that he is receiving from them "a treasure." The maternal uncle receives Rs.200/, the largest gift, because he stands as guardian in case of problems. These are token gifts only, symbolic, a Mizo Ph.D. candidate tells me, from the historic past. If a minor Christian girl becomes pregnant, the parents arrange for her marriage with the boy, under tribal law. [18]

A new step for the Catholic Church in India, brought about by the persistence of Catholic women's organizations, is the agreement of the R.C. bishops not to oppose the presentation to Government of a fresh bill for Christian Marriage and Matrimonial Causes. The bill would provide relief for the civil effects of marriages which have been annulled. After the annulment the case could go to the civil divorce courts, where the woman could look for financial and other relief. Also, a Women's Desk has been created by the Church, with a woman in charge, to consider women's causes. Catholic women are disappointed that the position is filled by a nun, not a lay woman, and does not have autonomous status, being a part of the commission for laity and family governed by a bishop. [19]

A young man studying in Madras for the Roman Catholic priesthood wrote to the editor of *Manushi*:

> I have been reading *Manushi* for the last two years. It is almost like a gospel for me. I read carefully, take notes, and return it to our college library .... I plan to study law after becoming a priest so that I am better equipped to combat the wrongs done to women. As you know, our theology itself is male-biased. Devotion to Mary is one reason for women's subjugation. I am now working

on a fairly vast topic, 'Women's Oppression in the Church,' in Tamil, my mother tongue. I use my Sunday sermons to speak about women and their problems.[20]

Another gem showing a sensitive male conscience, in letters to the Manushi editor, is from Ramdas of Hyderabad:

> I am a hypocrite like a good number of men but a watered down version, maybe. I remember trying to persuade my wife to visit **Manushi** and get to know more about herself and womanhood. She retorted. 1 have such a wonderful husband, why do I need to go there?' That was a big lie said to please me ... both of us knew the actual truth.
>
> Women are easily subjugated and taken advantage of because they love and care too much. It is a universal truth that women give of themselves more and sacrifice more .... Men get a lot more out of marriage than women. Invariably all women are happier before marriage than after. Men get sex, children (without all the labour), and not to forget, a cook, washerwoman, general handywoman, and someone who genuinely feels for him in all life's ups and downs and cushions him against hurts and disappointments. A tall order which a wife fills with ease .... God made women of sterner stuff but they suffer throughout life nevertheless, physically and emotionally .... It's a universal truth that softer, milder people are always taken advantage of and exploited. That's why men will continue to give women the raw end of the stick unless society wakes up and controls them ....
>
> Do you know why all well-known philosophers writers, scientists, inventors and composers are men? Because women were denied opportunity to decide their own course and were tied down with children and domestic affairs. If women were totally unfettered they would make better doctors, stateswomen, authors, bus conductors or whatever.
>
> The murder and mayhem one sees all over would be unthinkable if women were at the helm of public affairs. Can women maim and kill, rape and loot like men? Arrogance, vanity and ego are more pronounced in men. If mothers-in-law make impossible demands, it's because they are bad human beings who just happen to be women. The real fault lies with the cowardly, selfish son who allows his wife to be sacrificed thus.[21]

Thank you, Ramdas! What a challenge, to women and to men!

Contribution of Christianity

As I think of Indian Christian families with whom I have an ongoing relationship, one couple has just one daughter, three others have two, and three have three daughters. Surely all would have welcomed a son gladly, but I have never heard a word of regret, and they all have reason to be proud of their daughters. This does not speak for all Indian Christians, of course, but my experience is not uncommon.

This paper was to be about the abuse of India's Christian women. Abuse is there, unquestionably. But as we consider what their lives might be if the gospel had not come, we see how fortunate they are.

Education for girls came early to Christians through the work of women missionaries, with resultant job opportunities. In the early years of the nursing profession in India, 100 percent of the nurses were Christian. With the lessening of social taboos in areas of society, Christians now number about 50 percent of the nurses. But Christian girls paved the way. Many Indian women, including Christians, now are doctors. Many Christian women are school teachers. A 'first' in conservative church circles in Maharastra, where Protestants number only 0.15 per cent of the population, is the appointment of diminutive Miss Venu Ingle as Administrative and Academic Dean of coeducational Maharastra Bible College. She brought the school to an all time high with seventy students, and over fifty new student applications. Miss Ingle was a cross cultural missionary to Nagaland, then registrar and teacher in the Bible College, with fine seminary qualifications. She has counterparts in other Christian schools in India.

When we consider the standing that both the Word of God and the Indian Constitution promise women (voting rights at age 18, participation in government up to the highest office), we see only token progress; but the religious census has a story to tell.

The 1951 census showed such marked Christian growth in parts of the country that pressure came to restrict the issuing of visas to missionaries. I started watching later reports. We have noted the sharp decline in numbers of the female population, and I will lay it out for you here. For India as a whole, in relation to every 1000 males the ratio of females has been as follows:

    1901:**972**   1951:**946**   971:**930**   1981:**934**   1991:**929**   2001:**933**

Abortion was legalized in 1971, and abortion by sex selection through amniocentesis began in 1978. This shows in the census returns, which are tragic and greatly deplored. In 1978-83, 18,000 abortions of female fetuses were reported as performed following tests for sex determination. A survey in 1982 revealed that out of 8,000 abortions in six Bombay hospitals, 7,999 were female. In 1988 Maharastra State banned this use of amniocentesis. [22] A nationwide ban has followed, but is proving difficult to enforce. In India, to my knowledge, those Christians who seek to limit the number of their children do not resort to abortion.

The 1991 census had 994 Christian females to every 1000 males, 925 Hindu, 930 Muslim, and 888 Sikh females to every 1000 males.[23] The 2001 Indian census, total population of 1,028,610,328, shows still stronger contrast: **1009** Christian females to 1000 males, **931** Hindu, **936** Muslim, and **893** Sikh females to 1000 males.

For the nation, the 2001 census gave a literacy rate for age 7 and above of 64.8 percent. Christians had 80.3 percent, Hindus 65.1 percent and Muslims 59.1 percent. The literacy sex ratio showed Christian females at 8.2 percent below the males, Hindus 23 percent and Muslim females 17.5 percent below the males. I note that in States and Territories with a strong number of Christians – Kerala, Goa, Pondicherry, Daman, Mizoram, Andaman & Nicobar Islands – Hindus and Muslims showed their highest literacy rates. [24]

The population figures do not indicate increasing conversions of women, for Indian women rarely change their religion without their menfolk. Instead, the figures reveal the greater well-being of Christian women. Christian teaching imparts values for protective and nurturing relationships. Women as well as men are created in God's image, are heirs together of the gracious gift of life, and equally priests unto God (1 Pet.3:7, 2:5, Rev. 20:6). This equality will be clearly seen in the second, and major, portion of this little book. Christian law gives daughters equal inheritance rights with sons, and other protections. Widows do not lose dignity and worth, and if in need are to be cared for and not driven into penury and begging.

What shall we say about suicides and dowry deaths? The New Delhi police report that deaths in the city of about six women per day are dowry-related or suicides. The May 15, 1993 issue of the communist newspaper *Blitz* reported that in Gujarat, which it calls "decidedly the most saffronized state in the country, one woman commits suicide every hour to escape the consequences of being born in that sex. In the state, the suicide rate has gone up from one per day in 1953 to 25 per day in 1993."[25]

How many of the deaths were suicides and how many were murders, the newspapers cannot tell us. But that women are thought to be personally valueless and expendable, or whether they think of themselves that way, is a great tragedy and loss to us all.

Christians must earnestly teach the value our Lord placed on women in championing them, and teaching and challenging them spiritually, in his days on earth. Equally, Christians must live lives that proclaim those truths.

A slap to a woman may seem a love tap to her, but it is demeaning nonetheless if love can be shown that way. And the dowry evil that for the wealthy may seem a game and a conversation piece, is devastating to the lives of thousands of India's young, and to their parents. "To apply scriptural truth to every attitude and practice," as missionary Donna has said, would make Christians the people of God that India, and every nation, needs in their midst.

Looking Ahead

We envision in the new millennium the rise of Christian women for the strengthening of their own people and of the nation, especially its women and girls. India has had stellar role models, but must have many more. I cite two who have already been mentioned in this book.

Thangi Chhangte, who provided information on page 16, para 3, has returned to India's far northeastern hills with two masters degrees and a Ph.D in Linguistics. She is well into a rugged pioneer ministry of reducing to writing unwritten languages of Arunachal, developing primers and literacy materials in Adi, Nissi, and Apatami (with others to follow), training of translators, with the goal of developing literacy and native writers for tribal languages. So far only the Adi language has the N.T. Many thousands more wait to read God's Word. But now, in remote places where survey trips take her, eager small groups and great gatherings hear her preach that word.

Venu Ingle left a major work in Maharashtra Bible College to become Superintendent, in July 1998, of Ramabai Mukti Mission, Khedgaon. The multi-faceted ministry includes residential care and training for about 500 women and children, with church, school to 10th standard, a braille school, and a hospital with 10,000 outpatients and 300 surgeries last year. Due to lack of water the Mission now leases out its farm lands. Evangelists have outreach to a number of areas, and a few village churches and outlying boarding homes for boys and girls have been established. RMM has a hospitality ministry to visitors, and encourages prayer and financial support within India and from abroad. This large enterprise requires all of Miss Ingle's many abilities, and the dedicated, competent staff which God has provided.

Both of these women, and the Lord's many others whom they represent, deserve and need undergirding in prayer. Christians must raise their daughters to develop to their full potential, to be Christ's hands and feet of mercy and to share his Word.

Notes

[1] George Thomas Kurian. *The New Book of World Rankings.* 3rd ed. New York: Facts on File, 1991, p. 295.
[2] Statistics are from personal notes taken over the years from *The Times of India* and *Indian Express* newspapers, Mumbai. Government of India bulletin on The Religious Census. *The Statistical Outline of India 1992-93.* Mumbai: Tata Services Ltd., 1992.
[3] Personal letters from correspondents. Interviews. 1993-94.
[4] James and Phyllis Alsdurt. *Battered into Submission.* Downers Grove: InterVarsity Press, 1988.
[5] "Battered Women." *The Pioneer.* Lucknow: 29 March 1992.
[6] Kuruvilla Chandy. "Opposing the Dowry System. *Light of Life.* Mumbai: July 1993.
[7] Chandy. Letters to author. 18 September 1993 and 29 March 1994.
[8] Madhu Kishwar. "Inheritance Rights for Women." *Manushi, A Journal About Women and Society,* No.57. New Delhi: 1990.
[9] Edith Deen. *Great Women of the Christian Faith.* New York: Harper, 1959, p. 380.
[10] Kishwar. "Christian Law." Op. cit.
[11] Sarah Mathew. "Women Begin to Struggle Against Discriminatory Personal Laws." *Interaction, InterChurch Service Agency Quarterly,* Vol. 13. Chennai: 1990.
[12] M. J. Joseph. "Gendered Legislation and Justice." *National Council of Churches of India Review.* Nagpur: December 1993. "Christian Women's Rights in Kerala." *People's Reporter.* Bangalore: 15 January 1994.
[13] Kishwar. "What the Law Says." Op. cit.
[14] Kishwar. "Muslim Law." Op. cit.
[15] "Are Women Becoming an Endangered Species?" *Times of India.* New Delhi: 27 December 1988.
[16] *Indian Christian Marriage Act, 1872.* Lucknow: Eastern Book Co., 1992.
[17] *Indian Divorce Act, 1869.* Lucknow: Eastern Book Co., 1994.
[18] Thangi Changte. Interview with author. 17 January 1994.
[19] "Red Letter Day for Indian Christian Women." *People's Reporter.* Bangalore: 16-31 December 1993.
[20] "Letters." *Manushi,* No.73. November/December 1992.
[21] "Letters." *Manushi,* No.70. May/June 1992.
[22] *Times of India,* Ibid.
[23] India Network Archives: Census 1991 Information. 11 September 1997.
[24] "The First Report on Religion: Census of India 2001." *http://www.censusindia.net.*
[25] "Spare a thought for the oppressed Hindu woman." *Sunday Observer.* New Delhi: 23 May 1993.

Part 2

REMEDY
in 12 Biblical Studies on Equality of Man and Woman

Berkeley and Alvera Mickelsen

Preface

These study outlines have been worked out over a period of years as my husband, Berkeley Mickelsen, and I planned and team taught seminars on the subject of men/women relationships in many churches and conferences. Even before his sudden death in 1990 we planned to make the outlines available for others.

It is the study of the Bible itself that brings conviction, encouragement, and release from damaging traditions. Such traditions have often suppressed the freedom in Christ that his death and resurrection were meant to give to all believers, regardless of gender, class, age, or race.

Except for the first lesson, "Backgrounds for Sexual Discrimination," all lessons are basically a study of the Bible itself. Lesson 8, on the meaning of "head" in the New Testament, is based on my husband's intensive study of the Greek and Hebrew texts, in which he was highly skilled. While teaching he usually spoke directly from the text of the original languages. For the purposes of this book the New International Version is followed, except where otherwise noted.

These lessons can be used with a minimum of "teaching" by a leader. It is crucial for all to look up the scripture texts, read them in context, and discuss together their implications. In only a few cases have we suggested discussion questions. Discussion will arise automatically from the study.

A few suggestions:

1) Discourage "But I was brought up to believe that ...." Tradition is strong for all of us but it is not necessarily right! Let scripture challenge our traditions.

2) Encourage "What difference would this make in our homes and churches?"

May God enrich you as you study his Word on this important subject.

Alvera Mickelsen

1
BACKGROUNDS FOR SEXUAL DISCRIMINATION

I. The Old Testament was Written from the Perspective of a Patriarchal Culture.

A. Men were more valued than women; sons were more desired than daughters. Wives and daughters did not inherit from husbands or fathers. The priesthood was limited to men of the tribe of Levi.

B. In spite of this, some women were called by God to be leaders. Examples:

Deborah was a very successful judge and military leader (Judges 4, 5).

Huldah was the prophet who advised godly King Josiah and the high priest in an outstanding spiritual revival (2 Kings 22:1-23:25; 2 Chron. 34:1-35:19).

C. Nowhere does the Old Testament say that women are to be submissive to men or to their husbands, or that they should not be leaders or should be silent in public.

D. Proverbs 31:10-31 describes an ideal woman who is praised by her husband and children. She runs a business, buys and sells land, helps the poor, teaches her children.

Yet, by the time of Christ most Jewish rabbis interpreted the Old Testament to make women second class citizens or worse. Why? Possibly because the Jews were strongly influenced by the Greek thought around them. Rome had conquered the world militarily, but Greece had conquered it intellectually and philosophically.

II. Greek Disdain for Women Permeated Greek Society Long Before theTime of Christ.

Athens, the famous city state (500-300 B.C.), developed and taught the idea that women were in all ways inferior to men.

Homer (1000 B.C.): "each one gives the law to his children and wives."

Socrates (470-399 B.C.): "Woman is halfway between a man and an animal."

Plato (427-347 B.C.) wrote down Socrates' teachings.

Aristotle (384-322 B.C.) was a pupil of Plato and the most influential thinker of ancient times. "The most virtuous woman is crass in comparison to the basest male." He wrote his ideas in systematic form and formalized discrimination against women.

Zeno (c.334-262 B.C.) was the founder of stoicism, which taught that women tempt men away from a holy life.

III. Christian Era

Philo was a first century A.D. Jewish theologian who tried to harmonize the teachings of Plato and Aristotle with the Old Testament.

Josephus was a first century Jewish historian who studied Greek and Hebrew literature. He read Greek interpretations into the Old Testament. For example, he said the Jewish law declared wives inferior to their husbands in all things. [Not true.]

Tertullian (A.D. 160-230), famous influential preacher. "Women are the devil's gateway."

St. Augustine (400). "Marriage is a covenant with death."

Thomas Aquinas (1225-1274). "Woman is defective and misbegotten." He did the most to harmonize Aristotle's thinking with the Christian faith. Thus the Greek attitude toward women became thoroughly imbedded in Christian theology.

IV. Reformation Theologians

Martin Luther: Women and men were equal before the fall. After the fall women are forever subordinate because Eve sinned first.

John Calvin: Women were subordinate from creation. Proof: God created Adam first.

Roman Catholic thought was highly influenced by Augustine and Aquinas. The late Pope John Paul II held the view that women cannot be priests because they do not bear "physical resemblance" to Christ.

Note: Some of this material is from the book *What Paul Really Said About Women,* by John Temple Bristow, Harper and Row, New York, 1988, pp. 1-29.

2

HOW DO WE INTERPRET THE BIBLE?

I. Two Steps

A. What was God saying through his human servant to the first hearers and readers of this passage?

The Bible is an ancient book, written between 3000 and 1900 years ago, in Hebrew, Aramaic, and Greek. How can we possibly know what God was saying to those first hearers or readers, or what they understood it to say? Not easy, but there are definite clues we can get.

1. The context. What is the total message of a particular book or section of a book? Does the passage itself hint or spell out the situation in which the book was written? The book of Joel, for example, tells us clearly about a locust plague that had devastated the land. The book of First Timothy keeps mentioning false teachers and those who had departed from the faith. These are important clues in reading those books.

2. Secular literature, secular history, and myths often tell much about the problems, cultural patterns, customs and traditions of people in a certain place and period of history. This often sheds much needed light on parts of the Bible written to people who lived in those situations.

3. If we do not ask what the material meant to the first hearers or readers in light of their historical, cultural and religious situation, we rather assume that they did not count and that God was really providing the Bible for us in the 1990s. Appalling pride! When we ask *first* what it meant to the first hearers or

readers, we are kept from making ridiculous interpretations. It certainly is true that passages may have different applications for different periods in history, but let us not pretend that the God-inspired writer was writing primarily for us instead of for people of his own time. After we have asked what it meant for those first hearers or readers, then we are ready for the second question.

B. What does this passage say to us today? Does it apply to us? How do we know whether it applies to us?

1. This is where we need to look at all other texts in the Bible that deal with the same or similar topics or situations. If, for example, there are differences in what men and women should do in home, church, and society, we must examine **all** relevant texts, not just those that say what we want them to say.

2. What would make a particular text not apply to us? Perhaps our situation is entirely different and the reasons for the teaching no longer exist. But is this not dangerous? We can just say, "That doesn't apply to us." Yes, that is a danger, but it is even more dangerous not to ask these questions. If we don't, we will be caught in the practice of "selective literalism," choosing the texts that say what agrees with our ideas, and ignoring all others. This is why it is important to recognize two categories of teachings.

II. Two Categories

A. Highest norms or standards-principles taught in the Bible that must take first place in our considerations and have top priority in all that we do.

B. Regulations for people where they were.

All of the Bible is inspired by the Holy Spirit, and all is valuable to us for teaching, for reproof, for correction, and for training in righteousness so that everyone who belongs to God may be proficient, equipped for every good work (see 2 Tim. 3:16). It does not say that all is equally relevant for every situation. It says that we can learn something from all of it.

III. How Can We Distinguish Between Highest Standards and Regulations for People Where They Were?

A. Highest norms or standards were emphasized by Jesus (and often by Paul and other biblical writers) and were sometimes stated to be highest standards. Examples:

"In everything do to others what you would have them do to you; for this sums up the Law and the Prophets" (Matt. 7: 12).

"Love the Lord your God with all your heart and with all your soul and with all your mind." This is the first and greatest commandment. And the second is like it: 'Love your neighbour as yourself.' All the Law and the Prophets hang on these two commandments" (Matt. 22:37-40).

"Love your neighbour as yourself. Love does no wrong to a neighbour. Therefore, love is the fulfillment of the law" (Rom. 13:9b-10).

B. Sometimes highest norms are found in a single event and its effects. Bible evidence for Pentecost and its meaning as a highest norm or standard is provided by Joel, John the Baptist, Jesus, Peter, Paul. At Pentecost (Acts 2:1-18, 33) Peter quotes the passage in Joel 2:28 to show that the coming of the Holy Spirit transcends old barriers between Jews and Gentiles, males and females, young and old, servants and masters. All these barriers existed in Judaism, but Christ came that all might have life in him free from such barriers and divisions. The coming of the Holy Spirit was important to many of the biblical writers, and to our Lord.

1. Joel 2:28-29
2. John the Baptist: Matt. 3:11; Mark 1:6-8; Luke 3:16; John 1:26-34
3. Jesus: John 7:37-39; 20:19-23; Luke 24:46-49; Acts 1:48; 11:16
4. Peter: Acts 2:14, 14-18; 10:44-48; 11:15-18
5. Paul: Gal. 3:26-29

C. Sometimes highest norms are declared at the conclusion of an entire book. The Old Testament law teaches a complete order of sacrifices. Christians do not fulfill the O.T. sacrifices. Why? Because the book of Hebrews teaches that Christ himself was the perfect, ultimate sacrifice "once for all" (Heb. 10:8-18). Paul says the O.T. ritual was only "a shadow of the things that were to come; the reality, however, is found in Christ" (Col. 2:16-17, cf. Heb. 10:1-22).

D. Jesus himself and his teachings are the highest standard, as he made clear in Matthew 5:17. He came not to abolish the law and the prophets, but to fulfill them.

Anyone who looks closely at the life and teachings of Jesus knows that he did not follow the cultural custom of the Jews in treating women as subordinate. Women were among his disciples (although not among the twelve); he taught them the deep things of God. He even commanded them to teach men and committed to them the greatest message the world has ever known, his resurrection, to make it known to the disciples (John 20:18; Matt. 28:8-10).

E. A highest norm is found in Jesus' definition of true leadership and greatness when he rejected the Gentile "chain of command."

Jesus' teachings about authority and servanthood are contrary to the practices of the ancient world and of our modern world. "You know that the rulers of the Gentiles lord it over them, and their high officials exercise authority over them. Not so with you. Instead, whoever wants to become great among you must be your servant, and whoever wants to be first must be your slave; just as the Son of Man did not come to be served but to serve, and to give his life as a ransom for many" (Matt. 20:25-28; cf. Mark 10:41-45; Luke 22:24-27; John 13:12-16). It is interesting that in all of the instances in the Gospels where Jesus gave this important teaching it was always to the male disciples. Why? I don't know, but probably because women had already been socialized to be "servants." The male disciples had not been socialized in that way.

F. Sometimes highest norms are found in connection with what is involved in the change of covenant, orders, ages, etc. Luke 22:20; Jer. 31:31-34; 2 Cor. 3; Heb. 8:13; 9:13-14, 23-28.

Jesus explained this with a metaphor. "No one pours new wine into old wineskins; if he does, the new wine will burst the skins, the wine will run out and the skins will be ruined. No, new wine must be poured into new wineskins" (Luke 5:37-38).

Thus, the areas in which Jesus and the Gospels clearly broke with the practices and teachings of Judaism must be considered "new wine" and "highest standards" (Matt. 9:17; Mark 2:21-22; Luke 5:37-39; John 4:20-26).

IV. Regulations for People Where They Were

The Bible has many regulations for people "where they were." These appear in both the Old and New Testaments. The highest norm or standards back of some of them is apparent. For others, we cannot be sure why the regulation was given at the time, probably because we are too far removed in history and culture to understand the situation.

A. Old Testament examples. (There are hundreds of similar ones.) "Do not plant your field with two kinds of seed.

"Do not wear clothing woven of two kinds of material" (Lev. 19:19).

"Do not cut the hair on the sides of your head or clip off the edges of your beard" (Lev. 19:27).

B. New Testament examples:

The command in Acts 15:28-29 to all churches that Gentile converts were not to eat food offered to idols, blood (no rare steaks?), anything strangled, nor to indulge in unchastity. All these were extremely offensive to many Jewish believers in the churches who really felt that Gentile believers should keep all the Old Testament law. These Jewish believers felt that the command of the Jerusalem council was a compromise. Some of the new converts had come from Greek pagan religions and needed to be reminded that they were to break with the old practices. The only part that Christians still regard as important is the command of chastity, because that is enforced by the teachings of Jesus and other New Testament writers and is clearly in keeping with the highest ideals Christ taught.

There are others. Five times Paul and Peter wrote Christians to greet one another with a holy kiss. This is rarely practiced today. Paul's word to Timothy, "Stop drinking only water, and use a little wine for the sake of your stomach and your frequent illnesses" (1 Tim. 5:23), shows concern for Timothy's health, but can hardly be considered universal medical treatment for all times for all people who have digestive problems. Yet none of these commands were ever rescinded in the New Testament.

Any teachings in the New Testament that seem contrary to the highest norms and standards established by Jesus must be examined carefully to see whether local or temporary situations might be the basis for the apparent contraditions. Proper interpretation demands that *all* texts on any subject be examined in the light of sound methods of interpretation.

V. Common Faults in Bible Interpretation

A. Selective literalism: choosing a text that seems to say what you like and reading it literally, without regard to literary, historical, or cultural context. Then ignoring all other texts that seem to say the opposite. Example: Select Ephesians 5:22, "Wives submit yourselves to your own husbands as to the Lord," while ignoring verse 21 addressed to all Christians, men and women: "submitting yourselves to one another out of reverence for Christ." Ignore also 1 Corinthians 7:3-16 which teaches mutual submission and full equality of husbands and wives.

B. Reading into the text meanings that are not there. For example, read "male dominance" into Genesis 2:18 because the woman is said to be created as a "help" for the man. The Hebrew word for "help," *ezer,* is used in the Old Testament usually in describing God as our help. *Ezer* is not used in the Old Testament of a subordinate.

Faulty interpretation reads into Adam's creation prior to Eve's in Genesis chapter two the idea that males are therefore ordained of God to dominate females. The Bible neither says nor implies that. Actually, God frequently chose the younger persons for positions of leadership: Moses over Aaron, Jacob over Esau, David over the older sons of Jesse.

C. Propositional exegesis: asserting a proposition and then searching for texts by the above methods to support the propositions. By this method the Bible can be, and has been, used to *prove* almost anything the interpreter chooses.

God has given us the Bible as a guide to our lives and our thinking. It is important that we study for ourselves what the Bible says on the subject of man/woman relationships and on every other subject. We have access to the Bible and Bible study helps, and must not forget that "from everyone to whom much has been given, much will be required" (Luke 12:48b, NRSV).

3

GOD'S IDEAL AND HOW IT WAS DESTROYED BY SIN

I. Meanings of "Adam" (Same Hebrew Word for Humankind, Man, and the Name, Adam)

In Gen. 1:26, "man" (same word as Adam) means humankind. In Gen. 2:7 'man' refers to a single male.

In Gen. 5:1, "Adam" (or man), in the first part of the verse is the proper name for an individual. 'Man,' in the second portion, means humankind.

In Gen. 5: 2, "Adam" (or man as humankind) refers to the couple, Adam and Eve.

II. God's Purpose and Word for Women and Men (Gen. 1:26-31)

A. "Man" in Gen. 1:26 obviously refers to humankind.

B. Men and women equally bear the image of God (Gen. 1:27).

C. God gave to men and women the same responsibilities:

to be fruitful and multiply

to fill the earth and subdue it

to have dominion over every living thing

D. God was pleased with what he had created (Gen. 1:31).

III. The Creation Account in Genesis 2 Further Reveals God's Plan.

A. God made animals and Adam from "the dust of the ground" (Gen. 2:7, 19).

B. Adam became aware of a serious lack (Gen. 2:18-20). He was alone and did not have anyone "like him."

C. God created Eve from Adam's side and Adam immediately recognized that she was made of the same "stuff" as he, and fulfilled God's design to make a "helper fit for him" (RSV). "Fit for him" is defined in standard Hebrew English lexicons as "equal and corresponding to."

D. "Helper" in the Old Testament never indicates "subordinate" or "under the authority of." The Hebrew word ezer, translated help or helper, appears 21 times in the Old Testament. Most of the references are to God as our helper. When used of God the term ezer means "strength" or "power." In the few instances where ezer is used of someone other than God, the context indicates that the meaning is something like "ally." The proper description of Eve in Genesis 2:18 is "a strength or power or partner equal and corresponding to him." The 1989 New Revised Standard Version has "a helper as his partner."

IV. When Sin Entered the World God's Plan was Damaged (Gen. 3:3).

Sin damaged all the good relationships God had created:

    between people and God

    between people and nature

    between people and people – Adam and Eve

A. All statements addressed to Adam are equally applicable to Eve. To all men and women sin brought death, toil, and weeds (Gen. 3:17-19).

B. The statement addressed to Eve indicates that the mutuality that had existed between her and Adam was now damaged. Now, her husband would rule over her (Gen. 3:16). Despite this, the woman's "seed" would eventually destroy the serpent's (Satan's) power (Gen. 2:15). This refers to the birth of the Messiah, the Saviour of the world.

V. Answers to Some Interpretations of Genesis

A. Does God's creating Adam first (Gen. 2) indicate that males are meant to be dominant over females? The Bible gives no such indication. Although the Hebrews did give first preference to the firstborn. son, God's acts tended toward the opposite. God chose Jacob instead of Esau, his older twin, to be the ancestor of the Hebrews. God chose Moses, younger brother of Aaron, to lead his people from Egypt and to become the Great Lawgiver. God chose David, the youngest of Jesse's eight sons, to be the most prominent king of Israel and the ancestor of Christ.

B. Does Adam's naming of Eve indicate that males are to be dominant? The Bible never indicates special authority for the namer. Eve, not Adam, named Seth, their son. Rachel and Leah named the twelve sons of Jacob. Mary was told to name Jesus.

C. Is Genesis 3:16 ("he shall rule over you") a God-ordained command? No, it is the result of sin, not a God-chosen rule. It predicts what *would* happen, not what *should* happen. If everything in this section were "God-ordained" we should never pull up a thorn or thistle in our gardens (Gen. 3:18), nor use airconditioning. (We, specifically men, are supposed to "sweat.") (Gen. 3:19).

D. Are women forever doomed to carry the responsibility for sin in the world "because Eve sinned first"? There is enough blame to go around for us all. More important, Christ's atonement is sufficient for all women and men; we all are saved by grace through faith.

E. Was Eve's sin that she stepped out of her "role" and listened to Satan rather than be submissive to her husband?

This common teaching is clearly contrary to Genesis 3:17 which states that their sin was disobedience in eating the forbidden fruit, not in any "role reversal." Neither God nor Adam chided Eve for acting on her own initiative. This was not a sin on her part.

4

MEN AND WOMEN
IN THE OLD TESTAMENT

Note: The Hebrews of the Old Testament were strongly (but not exclusively) patriarchal in social organization, just as the nations around them were. Yet it is doubtful that the Hebrews considered their patriarchal society to be God-ordained, for there were many exceptions to the male-dominant practices, some of them involving women prophets. The exceptions will be considered here.

I. Both Men and Women were Temporal Leaders.

Judges, during one period of Israel's history, were the highest authorities in the land, called to their office by God (Judges 2:16-18). Examples:

Deborah was one of the most successful judges and was recognized by her people as God's spokesperson (Judges 4, 5). She was a prophet, military commander, wife, musician, singer, poet.

Gideon was a judge and military leader chosen by God (Judges 6:11-8:33).

II. Both Women and Men Played Crucial Roles in Liberating Israel from Egypt.

Examples:

The midwives who disobeyed Pharaoh (Ex. 1:1 5-22)

The **mother** and **sister** of Moses who helped save him (Ex. 2:1-10)

Pharaoh's daughter, who thwarted her father

Moses and **Aaron,** who led the Israelites out of Egypt (Ex. 3:1-4:16)

III. Some Women were Prophets, Although Most Prophets Were Men.

Examples:

Huldah, a contemporary of Jeremiah and Zephaniah (2 Kings 22:1-23:25; 2 Chron. 34:1-35:19). Huldah was influential in the revival under King Josiah. Both the king and the high priest recognized her as a prophet of God and came to her for help and advice.*

Deborah (see above), **Miriam** (Ex. 15:20-21), and the **wife** of **Isaiah** (Isa. 8:3).

IV. Both Men and Women Served in the Culture of the Community.

Examples: Men and women prepared the Tabernacle (Ex.3 5:20-29). Women and men together sang in the temple choir (2 Chron. 35:25; Neh. 7:67).

V. Care and Instruction of Children were Joint Responsibilities.

Fathers and mothers were to be honoured alike and listened to equally (Prov. 1:8; 6:20; 30:17; Deut. 5:16; 6:6-9, 20-25).

VI. In at Least Some Marriages Wives Participated Heavily in Decision-Making.

The **"ideal wife"** of Prov. 31:10-31 ran a business, a farm, a vineyard, a household of servants, did social work, was an effective teacher, and received the praise and support of her husband and children.

Hannah herself chose to dedicate Samuel to the Lord. (1 Sam. 1:9-11, 21-24).

Abigail saved her community, acting on her own initiative. (1 Sam. 25:2-28).

Sarah and **Abraham**. Note the tragedies that occurred when Sarah blindly obeyed Abraham instead of doing what was right (Gen. 12:11-20) and when Abraham obeyed Sarah instead of doing what was right (Gen.

16:2-6). However, in Genesis 21:12 Abraham is told by God to obey Sarah (see lesson 7). God spoke individually to Abraham, Sarah, and to Hagar (Gen. 18:10-15; 16:7-13).

VII. The Sexual Relationship in the Song of Solomon is one of Mutual Respect.

This exquisite love poem embodies concepts of mutual respect and delight in each other. See what they say about one another in 2:16; 3:1-6; 5:16; 7:10-13.

* Nehemiah's mention of the prophetess Noadiah, though not in a favourable light (6:14), is further evidence that the Hebrews recognized women prophets.

5

JESUS' ATTITUDE TOWARD WOMEN AND MEN

I. The Kind of World into which Jesus Came

A. Women were often forbidden to study the Torah (Old Testament). Girls did not go to the synagogue schools where boys were taught to read and write. Some rabbis said it was wrong to teach girls.

B. The testimony of women was not accepted in court unless a man could verify what the women said.

C. Women could not enter the Court of Israel in the Temple. It was reserved for men, and boys over age 12. Women were restricted to the women's court to which all Jews – men, women, and children – were admitted. Jesus chose to do his teaching in the Court of Women.

D. Women were not counted toward the quorum (often) required for a synagogue. In everything, women were counted as children.

E. Rabbis (teachers) never spoke to women in public, not even to their own wives or daughters.

F. Women did not normally inherit property from husbands or fathers. This is probably one reason why widow and poverty seem almost synonymous in the Bible.

G. Jewish women could not divorce husbands for any cause, but husbands could easily divorce their wives.

II. Jesus Tolerated No Double Standards.

A. John 8:1-11. The woman taken in adultery. (Lev. 20:10 says both parties were to be stoned.) Jesus appealed to the best in both the Pharisees and the woman.

B. Matt. 19:3-10. Teaching on divorce. Jesus refused to be caught up in the Pharisees' legalism. Rather, he called them back to God's plan for permanence in marriage. The disciples thought it then would be better not to marry!

III. Jesus Taught Women as well as Men, Contrary to the Culture.

A. Luke 8:1-3. Women travelled with and supported Jesus and the disciples.

B. Luke 24:6-9. The angel reminded the women of what Jesus had taught them. The teaching about his death and resurrection was "inner circle" teaching, not what they would have heard as part of the crowds who listened to Jesus' sermons.

IV. Jesus Corrected Erroneous Ideas of Both Men and Women and Never Patronized, Spoke Condescendingly, to Women.

A. Martha thought Mary belonged in the kitchen (Luke 10:38-42).

B. Peter thought Jesus should not talk of dying (Matt. 16: 21-23).

C. An anonymous woman in a crowd tried to pay Jesus and his mother a compliment (Luke 11:27-28). What in the compliment needed correcting?

D. James and John wanted to call down fire from heaven on some Samaritans (Luke 9:51-55).

E. Jesus opposed titles and privileges (Matt. 23:5, 12).

V. Jesus' Teachings and Miracles Treated Men and Women Alike.

A. Jesus often used adjacent illustrations, male and female. Examples:

Matt. 24:40 and 24:41

Matt. 13:31-32 and 13:33

Luke 15:3-7 and 15:8-10

Matt. 25:1-13 and 25:14-30

B. Women and men were treated alike in episodes of healing. Compare:

Mark 5:25-34 with Mark 10:46-52

Luke 13:10-17 with Mark 3:1-5

Luke 7:11-17 with Luke 8:40-56

C. Jesus used both women and men as examples of spiritual truths. Compare:

Mark 10:17-22 with Mark 14:3-9

Luke 18:1-7 with Luke 18:9-14

Mark 12:41-44 with Mark 12:13-17

John 12:1-8 with John 13:3-15

VI. Jesus Entrusted to Some Women and to Some Men the Most Important Spiritual Truths.

A. To the Samaritan woman at the well Jesus made the first clear announcement of his Messiahship. The Samaritan woman became the first recorded evangelist (John 4:7-42).

B. Peter's great confession that Jesus was the Messiah (Matt. 16:13-20).

C. The truths and example of the Last Supper were given to the twelve disciples (Luke 22:14-27).

D. Women were the first to see the risen Lord, and were told to take this great news to the disciples. Jesus did not choose to appear to Peter and John, although they also came to the empty tomb (John 20:1-18; Matt. 28:5-10; Luke 24:11-12).

E. Women apparently were important sources for the Gospel accounts (Luke 1:1-4). A large part of the Gospels is devoted to the birth, death, and resurrection of Christ. Much of the material in Luke 1-3 could have come only from Mary, the mother of Jesus. Details about the resurrection had to come from the women who went to the tomb. They were present also at the crucifixion, when all the disciples except John had fled (Luke 23:26-56; Matt. 27:5 5-56; Mark 15:40-47; John 19:25-27). Luke, Paul's companion, could have gathered this material during the Apostle's two year imprisonment in Caesarea (Acts 23-26).

VII. Men and Women Together Waited for and Received the Holy Spirit, and Proclaimed the Mighty Works of God.

Acts 1:8, 14; 2:1-21, 33; Luke 24:49; John 7:37-39; John 20:19-23.

6

WOMEN AND MEN IN THE EARLY CHURCH

I. New Testament Prophets Included Both Men and Women.
  A. Anna and Simeon (Luke 2:25-38)
  B. Men and women at Pentecost (Acts 1:14; 2:1-4, 17-18, 33)
  C. Daughters of Philip (Acts 21:8-9)
  D. Men and women in the church at Corinth (1 Cor. 11:4-5)

II. What is New Testament Prophecy?
  A. Edification, encouragement, comfort (1 Cor. 14:3-5)
  B. Evangelism (1 Cor. 14:22-25)
  C. Evaluation and teaching(1 Cor.14:26-32)
  D. Orderly presentation (1 Cor. 14:39-40)

III. Importance of New Testament Prophets
  A. They are recipients of the truths of God (Eph. 3:4-6)
  B. They are Christ's gift to the Church (Eph. 4:1)
  C. They and apostles are foundation of the Church (Eph. 2:19-20)
  D. They are appointed in the Church by God (1 Cor. 12:28)

IV. Women and Men were Among the Leaders of the Early Church.

A. Men and women both shared the persecution of the Church (Acts 8:3: 9:1-2).

B. Women in the church at Philippi

1. Lydia (Acts 16:13-15, 40). Apparently there were not ten Jewish men to form a synagogue in Philippi. Paul did not hesitate to join a women's outdoor prayer meeting as a base for his evangelistic efforts there. The church at Philippi began in Lydia's home, which became Paul's headquarters in that city.

2. Euodia and Syntche (Phil. 4:2-3). Paul describes these women as those "who laboured side by side" with him in spreading the gospel.

3. Philippi, Berea, and Thessalonica were in Macedonia (northern Greece) where women had more freedom and equality than in other parts of Greece. This is indicated in secular Greek literature, in archeological research, where we find statues erected in honour of prominent women, and in Acts 17:4, 12, where Luke mentions "prominent women."

4. The church at Philippi was one of Paul's favourites; he heaps praise on it in his letter to the Philippians. He says nothing in this letter or in the letters to the Thessalonians about women being silent in the church, or being subordinate, or not teaching, although these churches were in areas where women would be more likely to have places of leadership because the culture was more open to it.

C. Priscilla and Aquila (Acts 18:1-4; 18:24-28; Rom. 16:3; 1 Cor. 16:19; 2 Tim. 4:14). Paul says these two Christian leaders risked death to save his life. They had a church in their home wherever they lived, and they travelled from city to city. They were teachers of Apollos at Ephesus. Paul calls them his "fellow workers." In the Greek text, contrary to custom, Priscilla is usually mentioned first. This may indicate that she was the more prominent of the two in Christian activities, and came to mind first when Paul wrote about the couple.

D. Phoebe (Rom. 16:1-2). The Greek word describing Phoebe is *deacon*. Some English versions use "deaconess," although there was no such word in Greek literature at that time. Other translations use "servant."

This is an accurate translation, but should then carry the same meaning here as when used of church leaders in Philippians 1:1 and 1 Timothy 3:9, 12, and also in describing Paul, Timothy, Tychicus, and Apollos. It is the same word in all instances sometimes translated "minister." The other word used of Phoebe in Romans 16:2 is *prostatis*, the feminine form of the Greek word that means "leader, one who presides, stands before, patron." Some translations have used "helper, good friend, assistant," words that do not express the leadership flavor of *prostatis*. Paul is commending Phoebe in high terms, and she probably was the bearer of this epistle to the Romans.

E. In Romans 16:1-15 Paul mentions and sends greetings to ten specific women and seventeen men who apparently were well known and/or leaders in the church(es) in Rome. Although Paul had never been to Rome when he wrote this letter, he had heard about these people and sent personal greetings. He describes the women with the same terms he used for the men. The terms include deacon, protector, fellow worker, hard worker, apostle.

The name **Junias** in Romans 16:7 is considered by many scholars to be in error, and that it should be **Junia**, a woman's name. Until the 13th century it was so considered. Translators are thought to have changed it to Junias (even though no such male name has ever been found in the literature of that time) because they could not imagine Paul calling a woman an apostle. The RSV says in verse 7, "they are men of note among the apostles." The Greek text does not say "men." It merely days "they are of note among the apostles." The New Revised Standard Version makes the corrections. Phoebe is called a deacon and a benefactor. Junia is properly spelled as a woman's name, and she is "prominent among the apostles," in the general usage of the term *apostle*, missionary, as applied also to Timothy and Silas.

F. In 1 Corinthians 16:16 Christians are urged to submit to those who join in the work and labour at it, descriptions of Priscilla and Phoebe, as of the many men in positions of leadership in the early churches.

7

HUSBANDS AND WIVES IN MARRIAGE

I. Primary New Testament Teaching on Marriage Emphasizes Mutuality.

A. 1 Corinthians 7:1-16 is the only passage where Paul talks about marriage and nothing else. It deals with sexual relationships in marriage and with the spiritual effects of marriage partners on each other and on their children. Note that when Paul says, "I say, not the Lord" (v. 12 and by implication v. 6), it means that Paul did not have an oral teaching of the Lord Jesus on this point.

B. What differences does Paul indicate in attitudes of husbands and wives toward each other? What difference in influence of husbands and wives on each other or their children? What differences in responsibities? What similarities?

II. Compare 1 Timothy 3:12 with 1 Timothy 5:14.

Who is to rule or manage the household? Note the danger in taking either passage as an absolute statement.

III. How Did God Deal with Couples in the Bible?

A. Manoah and his wife (Judges 13:2-24). To whom did God appear and give instructions? Who showed the greater spiritual understanding of God?

B. Ananias and Sapphira (Acts 5:1-11). Whom did God hold responsible?

IV. Love Poem of the Song of Solomon

The entire book shows mutual respect, love, and initiative on the part of both lovers.

V. The "Ideal Wife" of Proverbs 31:10-31

She is a decision maker – a realtor, farmer, importer, teacher, entrepreneur, and manages a household of servants. Her children and husband praise her and call her blessed. Small wonder!

VI. Biblical Teachings About Submission Apply to all Christians.

A. Ephesians 5:21-33 begins, "submit to one another out of reverence for Christ." The next verse begins, "Wives, to your husbands." The word submit does not appear in the Greek text of that verse, but the meaning must be brought down from verse 21. The meaning of submit in verse 22 must be the same as in verse 21, where it refers to all Christians. Wives are to take its teaching about submission as seriously as the church takes its submission to Christ (see Appendix).

B. Husbands are to "give themselves up" for their wives as completely as Christ gave his life for the Church, in order to make completion possible for their wives just as Christ came to complete the Church (cf. Col. 2:10; 4:12). This is the meaning of husbands' headship in this passage. Husbands are to love and care for their wives as they do their own bodies. It is a headship of responsibility.

C. The emphasis in Ephesians 5 is on the *unity* of Christ and the Church and of husband and wife – not on any hierarchy. "For this reason a man will leave his father and mother and be united to his wife, and the two will become one flesh" (Matt. 19:5).

D. Submission and love are tied together and involve *all* Christians. See Phil. 2:2-8; Gal. 5:13-14; Rom. 12:9-10, 16; John 15:12-13.

VII. Wives are to Obey Husbands Like Sarah, Who Called Abraham Lord (1 Peter 3:17 NRSV).

A. The words "in the same way" (v. 1) refer to the preceeding passage in which Peter enjoins the willing submission of believers to their rulers and masters, even oppressive ones, which attitude Christ himself showed (1

Pet. 2:11-23). Peter then addresses women who might have non-believing husbands whom they want to win to the Lord. In "the same way" which he has just described, by willingly giving respect and service, with gentleness and a quiet spirit, they may win those husbands to share the faith that beautifies the wives.

The reference to Sarah calling Abraham lord is in Genesis 18:12, where she is speaking with the angel about the promise of a son in her old age. "After I have grown old and my husband (lord) is old, shall I have pleasure?" The obedience involved trying once more to conceive a son whom they both very much wanted, and which was in God's plan of sending the Saviour. Nowhere in the Old Testament is Sarah, or any other wife, told to obey her husband. Mutual caring would seek agreement. Genesis 18:5, where Abraham informs Sarah that unexpected guests have come, is simple house-hold communication, and he too took part in the preparations for showing hospitality. But on one occasion God told Abraham to obey Sarah (Gen. 21:12), although doing so caused Abraham grief. Ishmael had been born through the disobedience of unbelief; but this would not be allowed to hinder the faith covenant. Abraham obeyed, and sent away Hagar and Ishmael.

B. 1 Peter 3:7 warns husbands that their prayers will be hindered if they do not honour their wives as the weaker sex. In what way are women weaker than men? In many countries they live longer, are less subject to most diseases, have more endurance. But they are weaker in physical strength. Is this what Peter was talking about? Probably not. Most likely he was recognizing that in his day, as in ours, women have less power economically, socially, and politically; but that husbands and wives are joint heirs of the grace of God, and unless husbands honour their wives, their prayers will be hindered.

8

MEANING OF "HEAD" IN THE NEW TESTAMENT

The basic meaning of the word head in the New Testament is "extremity." The word head or heads appears about 50 times in the New Testament. Most of the references are to the physical head of a person.

There are, however, seven passages in the writings of Paul where he speaks of Christ as the head of the Church, and/or the husband or man (same Greek word) as the head of the wife or woman (same Greek word).

To know what Paul meant we must try to find out what head meant in the Greek language during the first century when Paul wrote those passages using the Greek word *kephale.*

The most comprehensive lexicon of the Greek language of that period available in English is one compiled by Liddeli, Scott, Jones, and McKenzie that covers classical and koine Greek from 1000 B.C. to about A.D. 600. The lexicon lists about 25 figurative meanings of head that were used in ancient Greek literature. The list does not include our common English usage of head as "authority over," "boss," "superior rank" or anything similar. Instead, the lexicon includes figurative meanings such as top or extremity of such things as a vessel, a wall, a capital of a column, the source or mouth or origin of something (we speak of headwaters of a river), the crown or completion or consummation of something. Sometimes head stands for the whole person.

The Hebrew word *rosh* (meaning head) was often used the way we use head in English to mean leader, ruler, authority over, and so forth. It appears with this meaning about 180 times in the Old Testament. In most of the other 400 and more times where it appears, *rosh* refers to a physical head. It is significant that when it meant physical head, the Septuagint translators used the Greek word *kephale*.

However, when the Hebrew word meant "leader, chief, authority over," the Septuagint translators nearly always used some other Greek word. Usually (109 times) they used *archon*, Greek for leader, instead of *kephale*, Greek for head. They used *hegeomai* (Greek for ruler) nine times, *protos* (Greek for first or foremost) six times, and several other Greek words a few times. *Kephale* appears four times when there is a head-tail metaphor where nothing else would make sense, but only eight times otherwise. Why did these early translators take pains to find substitutes for *kephale*? Apparently they realized that kephale (head) in Greek did not mean the same as *rosh* meant in Hebrew.

Since Paul was a Greek-speaking Jew (he grew up in the Greek-speaking city of Tarsus) with Greek as his native language, and since he wrote his epistles to Greek speaking churches in areas where most of the converts knew only Greek, he would likely use Greek with meanings that his readers clearly understood.

A careful examination of the seven passages where Paul used *kephale* in reference to Christ indicates that when they are read with common Greek meanings of *kephale*, we see a more exalted Christ than we see when we read head (*kephale*) primarily with the mistaken meaning of "authority over." When Christ is spoken of as the head of the Church, it may refer to him as the Church's source of life, as its top or crown, as its exalted originator and completer. These rich meanings are lost when we think of "authority" as the meaning for the word head.

There is no question but that Christ *does* have authority over the Church and over all the world, but that authority is established in other passages of the Bible such as Matthew 9:6; 28:18; and John 5:26-27.

Unfortunately, we are used to reading "head" with the English meaning of authority over. When we read references to man or husband as head of the woman or wife, we automaticaliy think "authority over." This misreading of the Greek meaning for head has been used to claim proof of God-ordained male dominance over woman, when Paul may have been saying something quite different.

PART TWO 53

Hebrew "*rosh*" and Greek "*kephale*"

The Hebrew word *rosh* (meaning head) occurs approximately 600 times in the Old Testament. Usually it means the physical head of a person or animal. However, in about 180 times *rosh* means chief man, chief city, chief nation, chief priest that is, leader of a group. In these instances the Hebrew word is used metaphorically in a way similar to the way we use the English word "head" to mean a leader or someone in authority. Basically, however, *rosh* means extremity.

The Greek word *kephale* (head) did not have this dual meaning. The Liddell, Scott, Jones, and McKenzie lexicon lists approximately 25 meanings of *kephale*. The most common are:

1. Physical head of a person's body, one extremity. Feet are the other extremity.

2. Metaphorical meaning of "head" with persons or things. Here we find:

   a. top or brim of a vessel

   b. coping (molded top) of a wall

   c. capital of a column

   d. source of a river

   e. mouth of a river

   f. source, origin, or starting point

   g. apex (anatomy: heart)

   h. base (anatomy: heart)

   i. top or crown of anything

   j. completion or consummation of something

   k. noblest part

   l. military band of men, right hand of a phalanx*

Note: The word has no common meanings that imply authority over, superior rank, chief, leader, etc. The closest meaning would be "top or crown." The figurative meaning of top, brim, capital, source, origin, extremity, crown, or completion are possible meanings of *kephale* in the New Testament.

Between 250 and 150 B.C., a group of about 70 Jewish scholars translated the Old Testament into Greek. This was the first known translation of any book from one language into another and is called the Septuagint, Greek for 70. How did they translate the Hebrew word *rosh* (head) when it meant chief or leader? If the Greek *kephale* had been commonly known to have that meaning, translators would surely have used it. This would have been simplest. But these skilled translators seemed to take pains to use words other than *kephale*, when possible.

They used fourteen different Greek words to translate the Hebrew *rosh* the 180 times when it meant chief or leader. They *always* used *kephale* when it meant physical head.

Here are the Greek words the Septuagint used when the Hebrew *rosh* (head) meant leader or chief:

1. *archon* (meaning ruler, commander, leader) 109 times

2. *archegos* (captain, leader, chief, prince) 10 times

3. *arche* (authority, magistrate, officer) 9 times

4. *hegeomai* (to be a leader, rule, have dominion) 9 times

5. *protos* (first, foremost*) 6 times

6. *patriarches* (father or chief of a race, patriarch) 3 times

7. *chiliarches* (commander) 3 times

8. *archiphules* chief of a tribe) 2 times

9. *archipatriotes* (head of a family) I time

10. *archo*, verb (rule, be ruler of) I time

11. *megs, megale, niega* (great, mighty, important) 1 time

12. *proegeomai* (take the lead, go first, lead the way) 1 time

13. *prototokos* (firstborn or first in rank) 1 time

14. *kephale* (where head can mean top or crown) 7 times

15. *kephale* (in head-tail metaphor) 4 times

16. *kephale* (where various manuscripts have different readings) 6 times

Why was *kephale* used so seldom when it would have been the natural word to use if the Greek term was commonly known to be leader or chief?

1. Translators recognized that *kephale* did not normally mean leader or authority over, so they used other Greek words which clearly expressed that idea.

2. In the seven times out of 180 when they did use *kephale* the context permitted the idea of top or crown to convey the idea of leader.*

Since the Septuagint translators recognized that the Greek *kephale* did not carry the Hebrew meaning of leader, authority, or superior rank, we must be sure that we do not read our similar English meaning of head into the text. The following paragraphs will demonstrate other meanings.

* John Temple Bristow, op.cit. p. 37 says kephale was also a military term referring to the first one into battle. This is a possible meaning of the usages marked with asterisk in the above two lists.

Meanings of *kephale* (head) when used metaphorically by Paul

I. Colossians 1:18 (context 1:13-20)

Head = Exalted originator and completer.

Context: Who is the Christ in whom we have redemption?

Meaning of head in this passage (v. 18): he is the "head" (originator and completer) of the body, the Church. **Support** in context for this meaning: Christ is the beginning or first cause (v. 18). God reconciles all things to himself through Christ (v. 20).

II. Colossians 2:19 (context 2:16-19)

Head = Source of life.

Context: Warning about various heretical teachings.

Meaning of head here: "...has lost connection with the Head [source of life] from whom ...." **Support** in context for this meaning: the 2:19 prepositional phrase "from whom." Christ is the source of life from whom all the body grows.

III. 1 Corinthians 11:3 (context 11:2-16)

Head = Source as base.

Context: Hair style and hair covering when praying or prophesying in a public gathering. **Meaning** of head here: "the head [source] of every man ... [source] of woman ... [source] of Christ ...." **Support** in context for this meaning: "because man is not from the woman but woman from the man, so also the man is *through* the woman; indeed, all things are *from* God" (1 Cor. 11:8, 12).

IV. Col. 2: 10 (context 2:8-15)

Head = Source of life, and top or crown.

Context: Warning against philosophy and human tradition.

Meaning of head here: "... who is the head [top, crown] over every power and authority" (v. 10). **Support** in context for this meaning; believers have been made complete in relationship with Christ [vv. 11, 14]. Christ defeated evil demonic powers on the cross; disarmed and exposed them; triumphed over them.

V. Ephesians 1:22 (context 1:15-25)

Head = Top or crown.

Context: A prayer of Paul for his readers.

Meaning of head here: God "appointed him [Christ] to the church to be head [top or crown] over everything for the church." **Support** in context for this meaning, verses 20-22. Christ is at God's right hand, *above* all beings, all things *under* his feet, he is *over* all things.

VI. Ephesians 4:15 (context 4:11-16)

Head = Source of life.

Context: Gifts or gifted people are to build up the body of Christ.

Meaning of head here: "... we are to grow up into him in every way who is the head [source of life], Christ, from whom the whole body ... makes bodily growth and upbuilds itself in love" (RSV). **Support** in context for this meaning: verse 16, prepositional phrase "from whom" growth comes.

VII. Ephesians 5:23 (context 5:18-23)

Head = One who brings to completion.

Context: What it means to be filled with the Spirit; instructions to husbands.

Meaning of head here: "The husband is the head [enabler] of the wife as Christ is head [enabler] of the church ...." **Support** in context for this meaning: "Christ loved the church and gave himself up for her, to make her holy, cleansing her ... to present her to himself... radiant.... In this same way husbands ought to love their wives."

9

REGULATIONS FOR PEOPLE WHERE THEY WERE IN CORINTH

I. Problems in the Corinthian Church

A. Divisions in the church (1 Cor. 3:3-9): immorality (5:1-2); lawsuits (6:1-6); disorder (1 1:20-22); eating food offered to idols (8:1-13).

B. Sexual ambiguity as seen in hair styles. Long fancily groomed hair on males brought suspicions of homosexuality; homosexual acts were frequent in Corinth (see 1 Cor. 6:9-11). This port city, with 1000 temple prostitutes, was noted for licentiousness. The prostitutes wore their hair short, close-cropped; and Roman law said that women guilty of adultery were to have their heads shaved. This may explain Paul's obsession with hair and hair length in this chapter.

C. Since Pentecost had established that women and men were to pray and prophecy publicly (Acts 2:14-18), Paul wanted them not to blur their sexual identity as men and women when they did so, especially in light of the social climate at Corinth. They were to look moral as well as act morally.

D. Goddess cult worship in Corinth was prominent, had strong following among women, and was noisy, disorderly worship often involving cult prostitutes.

II. How Men and Women were to Pray and Prophesy in Public Gatherings (1 Cor. 11:3-16).

There is no Greek word for veil or unveiled in the text. The literal meaning of the words usually translated "veil" is "having it down from the head." It could mean veil, but since hair and hair length are so much discussed in this section, it may refer to a long hair style for the women. Jewish men always prayed with some head covering, and Paul himself would not consider that a dishonour (vv. 4, 7). But he was now addressing men of Corinth, with their different background.

A. Women needed some covering (long hair or veil) since they are the glory or splendour of men. Their attractiveness brought honour (splendour, glory, worth-enhancement) to the husband. Further, it was a kind of "mantle" for them, a sign that Pentecost gave them the right to prophesy (vv. 7-9, 13-15). In the Old Testament a mantle was a sign of a prophet.

B. Angels' concern for order (1 Cor. 11:10). Literal translation: "On account of this, the woman ought to have authority on the head because of the angels." (Did Paul have Isaiah 6:2 in mind?) "Authority" may mean a sign of authority (to prophesy) perhaps a hair style or veil. Some translations (TEV, Living Bible, Phillips) say she should have a sign that she is under her husband's authority; but the Greek text says nothing about a man or husband. The text seems to speak of her own authority or right.

C. The source and authority of men and women indicate their equality and interdependence. Woman was created from man, but now all men are born through women, and all things are from God (vv. 1112).

D. Because of the common meanings of "head" in the Greek language and because of the content of the rest of the passage, with its emphasis on origin or source, "head" in verse 3 seems to mean source, base, or derivation. (See lesson 8 on "head" for detailed explanation.)

III. Creativity in Church Services Should Not Bring Dishonour (1 Cor. 14:26-40).

A. Each member could participate in a variety of ways (v. 26).

B. Regulations would avoid confusion (1 Cor. 14:27-33).

1. **Tongues**: Only two or three should speak in tongues, and someone must be able to interpret. If there is no interpreter, the person with the gift should remain silent.

2. **Prophecy:** Two or three may prophesy in turn. Others should pass judgment, weigh what is said. God brings peace, not confusion. "You can all prophesy one by one so that all may learn and be encouraged." (Prophecy apparently involved a teaching function (see 14:3.)

C. Paul says that women should be silent in church, even though he has just written how both men and women were to pray and prophesy (11:4-16). There are at least two possible explanations for this passage (14:34-38).

1. Paul may have been telling wives not to interrupt services by asking questions of their husbands. (The Greek word for woman is the same as for wife.) If so, Paul may have meant that:

   a. Christian women should subject themselves to Paul's regulations that were on a par with Old Testament law (vv. 34, 37-38). But here is no O.T. law about women being silent in public or being subordinate. Or "the law" might refer to some Roman or Greek law prohibiting women from speaking in public.

   b. Their husbands should teach them at home and women should ask their questions at home (v. 35).

   c. Do the Christians at Corinth think they are the exclusive source of the word of God, that they have features no other church has (v. 36)?

2. Paul may have been quoting Judaizing teachers who opposed him in Corinth and who sought to prevent women from praying audibly, prophesying, or questioning in a church gathering. (The ancient Greek text included no question marks or punctuation of any kind. Translators have had to decide where Paul was quoting and where he was writing on his own. Therefore, absence of quotation marks in translations proves nothing. By setting verses 33b-36 as a separate paragraph, marked not with quotation marks but with parenthses, the NRSV indicates that Paul may have been quoting false teachers). He may have meant that:

   a. Teachers, in verse 34, were quoting Jewish oral law in saying that women should be silent, and that

   b. they should learn from their husbands at home (v. 35).

   c. Paul answers: Do you, as one group in Corinth, think that only you have the word of God (v. 35)?

    d. He defends his authority to teach the word of God even when it runs contrary to the Jewish oral law (vv. 37-38).

We are too far removed from the cultural and historical situation to know for certain exactly what Paul was dealing with and why. We do know that his own approval of Priscilla as a teacher of Apollos, his instructions about how women were to pray and prophesy, and his knowledge of the affirming ministry and attitude of Jesus toward women make his disapproval of women participating extremely unlikely.

10

REGULATIONS FOR PEOPLE WHERE THEY WERE IN EPHESUS

I. Problems in the Churches at Ephesus

A. False teaching (1 Tim. 1:3-20, NRSV)

1. "Certain people" (vv. 3, 6-7, 20) refers to both men and women.
2. Different doctrines, genealogies, that promote speculation (v. 4).
3. Two who had departed from the faith (vv. 19-20).
4. Importance of holding faith in good conscience (v. 5).
5. Gnosticism, the most serious group of heresies in the early church, was beginning to appear (1 Tim. 4:3; 6:20 2 Tim. 3:1-9). One branch of Gnosticism taught that Eve was created before Adam and was the one who enlightened him spiritually. Other Gnostic heresies taught that women should not marry and bear children, even that it was a sign of spiritual enlightenment to leave their husbands.

B. Immoral ifestyles (2 Tim.2:8-15)

1. Men who used prayer to air their quarrels and anger (v.8).
2. Women who did not pray in proper attire and with modesty and chastity (v. 9). Their expensive garb, with gold, pearls, elaborate hairstyles, gave wrong impressions. Ordinary Greek women were not likely to dress that way. That was the dress of the *hetaerae* (well educated Greek women who were often

the teachers and companions, often sexual, of Greek men). Perhaps some of these women were converts and were wearing suggestive clothing to church.

Syncretism (mixing of pagan and Christian ideas) has always been a problem for the church. It was present in the early church as seen in Revelation 2:14, 20-23. Paul says that some of the churches (located in Asia Minor and not far from Ephesus) were actually teaching Christians to practice immorality.

II. Paul's Advice Under these Circumstances

A. Women were to be learning quietly rather than teaching (1 Tim. 2:11).

B. These women were to be "learning in subjection" -to what or to whom? Perhaps to God, or to the teachings of the gospel, or to Timothy, their teacher.

C. These women were not to "have authority" over men. The Greek word here is *authentein* not the usual *exousia* used elsewhere in the New Testament for "authority." *Authentein* appears nowhere else in the Bible and is rare in Greek literature. It basically means "to thrust oneself" and usually had a negative and often sexually orientated meaning. There is some evidence that it could even mean "to claim to be the originator of." John Chrysostom (A.D. 4th century) translated it "sexual license."

D. Possible interpretations of this passage.

1. Paul was illustrating that women needed to be learning. Eve was an example of a sinless woman who met false teaching unprepared. She did not realize that she was sinning, although Adam did realize that he was (2 Tim 2:14). In spite of this, Eve (and these women in Ephesus likewise) would be saved through the godly posterity that centered in Christ (Gen. 3:15; Gal.3:16, 19, 29) if they respond with faith, love, and sanctification, with chastity (v. 15). The persistent emphasis on chastity in this passage may indicate some of the problems of the women about whom Paul was writing.

2. It is also possible that Paul was refuting one of the heresies of some gnostics who taught that Eve was created first and had some secret knowledge that Adam did not have. Perhaps some of the women were even teaching this. 1 Timothy 2:15 may also be a refutation of the gnostic teaching that a godly woman should not marry and bear children.

III. Qualifications of Bishops and Deacons (1 Tim. 3:1-12)

Both bishops and deacons are required to be "the husband of but one wife" (vv. 2, 12). It was previously thought that polygamy was nonexistent in the first century, but more recent research indicates that some men did have two or three wives, and quite possibly Paul here was ruling out polygamous men. The emphasis is on the moral and spiritual qualities of the officers, not on their gender. There is little doubt that the vast majority of church leaders in the first century were men, for most women had very little education or opportunity to develop.

1 Timothy 3:11, NIV reads, "In the same way their wives [variant, "deaconesses"] are to be women worthy of respect ...." The NRSV gives as variant reading: "Women deacons likewise must be ...." [See chapter 6, IV. D.] This was a very personal letter from Paul to Timothy, not a letter addressed to the church. Timothy would know by Paul's actions that his comment "husband of but one wife" was not intended to rule out qualified women as deacons. Paul had consistently affirmed Christian women.

IV. Highest Norms and Standards

A. This regulation for people "where they were in Ephesus" must be read in the light of the highest norms and standards taught by Christ and at Pentecost ("your sons and your daughters shall prophesy," meaning evangelize, preach, teach), and Paul's own acts in commending Priscilla, Phoebe, and other women leaders, including Euodia, Syntche, and Lydia.

B. These short phrases from 1 Timothy have often been used to justify keeping women out of all positions of leadership in churches. Doing this repudiates the highest norms and standards clearly taught by the Lord Jesus Christ and the Apostle Paul in other passages. It is selective literalism, selecting certain passages to be applied literally while ignoring others that teach differently. It is also an example of taking a passage out of its literary and/or historical context and thus failing to ask what it meant to the first hearers or readers before asking what it means to us today.

V. What Might these Passages Mean for Us Today?

A. In light of the literary and historical contexts, and in light of the highest norms and standards taught in the Bible, we would interpret 1

Timothy 2:11-15 as emphasizing the importance of Christians being adequately taught in the Scriptures before they become teachers.

It means that the church should always be alert for false teaching in any form. It means also that it is good and noble for women to marry and rear children.

B. We can be very sure that this passage was not a prohibition against all women teachers of all times. Priscilla, who is always commended by Paul, had been a teacher of Apollos earlier in this same city, and Apollos had gone on to become a great power for God in the early church. Timothy, the recipient of this personal letter, knew about Priscilla and Apollos and no doubt would never have thought Paul's words a prohibition against Priscilla and other women who worked closely with the Apostle. Paul knew that Timothy understood very well what he was writing about, and thus he did not need to spell out the details of the situation in Ephesus. Understanding would be easier for us if he had!

11

TEACHING ABOUT AUTHORITY IN THE BIBLE

I. God Alone is the Ultimate Authority for Every Person

...from the Garden of Eden to the end of time. Adam and Eve both were responsible for their disobeying God. Peter with the other apostles said, "We must obey God rather than men" (Acts 5:29).

II. Patterns of Earthly Authority Among the Hebrews were Generally Similar to those of the Surrounding Nations.

  A. Nations around Israel had kings. Israel wanted a king, and although God disapproved, he permitted them to have a king. I Samuel 8:5-22.

  B. Hebrews had slaves. Nations around them practised slavery.

  C. Many Hebrews regarded their wives as possessions, like men of the nations around them. They practiced polygamy like the nations around them.

  D. Age carried authority. Oldest persons in the family had authority; the firstborn had special privileges and responsibilities.

III. God did not Operate within those Authority Frameworks.

There is little or no evidence that the Hebrews thought that slavery, polygamy, kingship, or patriarchy as institutions were ordained of God even though the law of Moses gave explicit directions about the treatment of slaves, second wives, etc. For this reason the Hebrews were able to accept, apparently with little or no difficulty, the acts of God that ran contrary to their cultural patterns. God frequently chose the younger rather than the older for leadership and authority (i.e. David, youngest son of Jesse as king; Moses rather than Aaron, to lead the Israelites out of slavery. God sometimes chose women as spiritual and/or national leaders (i.e., Deborah as judge; Huldah as prophet).

IV. Word Pictures of God in the Bible are Often Based on the Societal Structures of that Day.

The use of such word pictures does not mean that those specific authority structures were ordained of God.

A. God is said to be king, believers are his subjects (Rev. 17:14; Psa. 47:2-7). That does not prove the "divine right of kings."

B. God and Christ are pictured as Master, believers are their slaves (1 Cor. 7:22-23; Col. 4:12; Rom.6:22). This does not prove that slavery is right, although that argument was used by some Christians.

C. God is pictured as husband, believers as wife. In the Old Testament God is husband, Israel is his wife. In the New Testament believers are "the bride of Christ" (Mark 2:18-20; John 3:29; 2 Cor. 11:2; Rev. 21:9). These terms do not indicate divine authority of husbands or God-ordained leadership by them over wives.

V. Jesus' Teachings about Leadership and Authority Run Contrary to Cultural Patterns.

Jesus had full and final authority to forgive sins (Matt. 9:6; Mark 2:10; Luke 5:24), and had all other authority in heaven and on earth (Matt. 28:18). Yet he taught and demonstrated that true leadership involves leading by example and serving and empowering others for service rather than exercising power over them (Matt. 20:25-28; 23:10-12; Mark 10:42-45; Luke 22:25-27; John 13:12-17; Gal. 5:13; 1 Peter 5:2-3).

VI. Christians' Concepts of Leadership and Authority Must be Based on the Teachings and Example of Christ and on the Highest Standards as Taught in the Bible.

A. Every person is created in the image of God and is ultimately responsible to love God and obey him above all others (Gen. 1:27; John 14:15; 1 John 5:2).

B. God is no respecter of persons and shows no partiality (Acts 10:34; Rom. 2:10-11; Gal. 2:6; Eph. 6:9). Christians are forbidden to show partiality (James 2:19).

C. In Christ there is neither Jew nor Gentile, slave nor free, male nor female (Gal. 3:28; Eph. 6:9).

D. All believers are called to servanthood and submissiveness. We are called to serve God and those around us by empowering them to serve God and others. Desire for power over others is a basic contradiction of the life and teachings of Christ (Luke 22:24-27).

E. Christ said that what we do to each other we are doing to him (Matt. 25:40-45; Acts 9:4-5).

F. We are called to be "a new creation," to be samples of the kingdom of God (2 Cor. 5:17). "The old has gone, the new has come!" See also Galatians 6:15. In 1 Peter 5:2-3 elders are told to lead by example, not by domineering.

G. The Golden Rule summarizes the highest standard for believers under both the Old and New Testaments. "So in everything, do to others what you would have them do to you, for this sums up the Law and the Prophets" (Matt. 7:12, RSV; cf. Luke 6:31).

VII. True Authority is Never Imposed on Others.

Demand for conformity can be imposed, but that is not true authority. Authority is given by others in response to the true leadership and servanthood that has been demonstrated. We love Christ because he first loved us. We respond to him because he has demonstrated his love and care for us. Our love and acceptance of his authority is freely given. He does not impose it.

12

THE GIFTS GOD GIVES TO BELIEVERS

I. Gifts Result from the Activity of God the Father, God the Son, and God the Holy Spirit.

1 Corinthians 12:4-6: "There are varieties of gifts, but the same Spirit; and there are varieties of services, but the same Lord; and there are varieties of activities, but it is the same God who activates all of them in everyone" (NRSV).

II. Gifts are Given to Every Christian, Without Apparent Regard for Economic Status, Racial Background, Age, or Gender.

Lists of gifts appear in three letters of Paul: 1 Corinthians 12:4-11, 28-30; Romans 12:3-13; and Ephesians 4:11-14. The lists are not the same, and obviously none of them is all inclusive. There are no doubt spiritual gifts that are not in these lists, such as music, the ability to be a sympathetic listener, and many others.

III. All Gifts are Given for the Same Purpose: To Build up the Body of Christ (Ephesians 4:11-17).

   A. Four specific purposes are listed:

     1. For the common good (1 Cor. 12:7)

     2. For building up of the church, and edification (1 Cor. 12:7; 14:26)

3. Making service effective, contributing to the growth of all (Rom. 12:3-13)
4. Equipping the saints for ministry (Eph. 4:11-14)

B. The list in Ephesians 4 includes prophets, and there are several references to women prophets in the New Testament. There is no indication that women are excluded from other categories in this list or in the other lists of gifts. The analogy of the church to the human body is presented more fully in 1 Corinthians 12:12-27, where Paul emphasizes the interdependence of the parts of the body, the church, and how it suffers when any part of the body suffers or is not doing what God has gifted it to do.

IV. Clarifications

A. Nothing is said about how many gifts people have. Paul had the gift of prophecy, of teaching, of healing, of tongues, and more.

B. Is there any reason to distinguish between gifts and talents?

C. Any reason to classify closely? Some gifts seem to overlap.

V. Exercise of Gifts

A. Paul gives regulations for gifts of prophecy and tongues in 1Corinthians 14.

B. "Gifts" do not preclude preparation (Col. 3:12-17; Eph. 5:18-21).

C. Relationship of gifts and grace in 1 Peter 4:9-11.

Appendix

J. A. McNally

Chapter 7, VI

The concise, valuable presentation by the Mickelsens should be an eyeopener to many, but may still leave questions. John Temple Bristow's book, previously referred to, treats extensively of the crucial Ephesians 5:21-33 and we quote, with his kind permission. Bristow comments that a close study of Paul's words reveals that the apostle was writing *against* the concept of male superiority, not defending it. "In the Greek, 47 words are directed at wives while 143 are directed at husbands."

Key Word: Be Subject To

Addressing the wives, the apostle used a form of the Greek word *hupotasso* which Bristow says in its active form might be used of a conqueror concerning the vanquished. It means "to subject to," "to subordinate."

"But," says Bristow, "Paul did not use *hupotasso* in its active form to describe any person .... He did not tell husbands to *hupotasso* their wives .... Instead, Paul used used this word in addressing wives only in its imperative, middle voice ... in the imperative mood hé was instructing wives... not describing them (as Aristotle did when he claimed that the male is by nature fitter to command than the female) .... he was appealing to them. In ... the middle voice form he was emphasizing the voluntary nature of being 'subject to'."

Greek and English both have the active and passive verb voices; but English does not have the middle voice which the Greek has, in which the subject acts upon the subject.

"And yet," Bristow explains, "we think in ways that the Greek verb form expresses. For example, a person may teach – an active verb. And one may be taught, a passive verb. But a person may also teach himself or herself by careful listening, discovering, reasoning, learning. In that sense the person is both subject and object of the action. That is what the Greek middle voice expresses, a voluntary action by the subject of the verb upon the subject of the verb.

"Now, it would be possible in Greek to tell a person to subject someone else (although Paul never did so); and it would be possible to describe someone as being subject to another. But one cannot tell another to be subjected,, any more than one can tell someone to be learned. However, Paul used *hupotasso* in the middle voice. This way, he was requesting that wives voluntarily, willingly, actively be subject to their husbands. This is the form *hupotassomai* (hoopotassomy). Since it is asking for something that is voluntary in nature, 'be subject to' is an awkward translation at best. *Hupotassomai* means something like 'give allegiance to,' 'tend to the needs of,' 'be supportive of' or 'be responsive to' ....

"There is in addition another meaning to *hupotassomai*. It also served as a military term, referring to taking a position in a phalanx of soldiers. In this sense there is no reference to any idea of rank or status—it was an equal sharing of the task for which the soldiers were ordered. If a soldier failed to join the others, or held back during an advance, a captain might use a form of the verb *hupotassoinai* to order him to return to the line, join his fellows, be supportive of them, fulfill his part of the assignment.

"In that sense Paul could tell all the members of the church to be subject to *(hupotassomai)* one another, and he could also tell wives to be subject to their husbands. For *hupotassomai* is not a ranking of persons as ruler and ruled. It is a concise appeal for the church to have its members live out their call to be 'the body of Christ and individually members of it' (1 Cor. 12:27; compare Rom. 12:15-16; 1 Cor. 10:16-17; Eph. 4:4, 16; Col. 1: 18), to be willing to 'bear one another's burdens and so fulfill the law of Christ' (Gal. 6:2). What is true of the church, Paul added, is to be true of a marriage."

Key Word: Love

In stressing that husbands are to love their wives, Paul does not use the word *eros* (romantic love), or *phileo* (for fondness, friendship, a deep liking), none of which can be ordered into being. The word he uses is *agapao* which Bristow calls:

"...not so much a matter of emotion as attitude and action .... and because it focuses upon a person's attitudes and actions, one can be asked to *agapao* someone. The great commandments used this word, telling us to love God and to love our enemies. And Jesus defined this word in his parable of the good Samaritan .... *Agapao* is almost identical with *hupotassomai*. Both involve giving up one's self interest to serve and care for another's. Both mean being responsive to the needs of the other. And both are commended to all Christians, as well as to husbands and wives."

Parallelism is a feature in the Hebrew language. Paul used the two key words in such parallel fashion. Wives are to *hupotassoinai* their husbands; husbands are to *agapao* their wives.

Bristow finds that "be supportive of" may be the most suitable translation of *hupotassoinai* in the Ephesians passage, and "be responsive to the needs of," for *agapao*, "so long as that phrase does not imply weakness on the part of the recipient or grudging charity on the part of the benefactor. After all, Jesus used this same word in his commandment that we love God."

Says Bristow, "Husbands are to be head of their wives not to lord it over them, but to love them and serve them, just as wives are to be supportive of their husbands." It is a protective, caring, responsible headship, denoting the husband as "spearhead, the first into battle." (*What Paul Really Said About Women,* pp. 35, 38-45. New York: Harper and Row. 1988.)

Chapters 9, III and 10, II
Key Word: Silence

The Apostle in chapter 11 of 1 Corinthians acknowledged and approved women's praying and preaching in church, but in 14:33b-35 seems to be writing in contradiction, saying that women should be silent. The context is orderliness in public worship. Understanding is needed about the words he chose, translated "silence" and "speak." Bristow explains a number of words. One is *phimoo* (*fim-OH-o*), which he says "... is often used to describe a kind of forced silence, perhaps best translated by our English idiom 'shut up' .... It describes how Jesus' answer to their question silenced the Pharisees (Matt. 23:34).... Jesus used *phimoo* also as a command, to quiet the unclean spirit that he cast out of a man (Mark 1:25; Luke 4:35) and to still the raging wind and sea (Mark 4:39) .... When Paul wrote that women are to be silent he did not use *phimoo* ....

"Instead, Paul chose the Greek word *sigao* (sigaho) .... a voluntary silence. It was used to describe the decision of th disciples to remain silent about the transfiguration they had just witnessed (Luke 9:36),... to describe Jesus' silence during his trial before Pilate (Mark 14:61) .... as when the multitude accompanying Jesus told the insistent beggar to quit yelling (Luke 18:39),... the kind of silence asked for in the midst of disorder and clamour. And Paul asked the women of the church [unused to their new freedom] to keep that kind of silence.

"Greek has many words that can be translated 'speak.' Five denote preaching or proclaiming, and twenty-five others can be translated 'say,' 'speak,' or 'teach.' Paul did not write that women are not to preach, or teach, or declare,... Instead, Paul wrote that women are not to *laleo* (*la-LA Y-o*). Like the other verbs, *laleo* can denote the act of saying something quite important. But of all the verbs that can be translated 'speak,' only *laleo* can also mean, simply, 'talk.'

"If someone wished to write in Greek 'please do not talk during the prayers,' the verb would have to be *laleo*. Since Paul's instructions were given to a congregation troubled with tumult and discord during the worship services, he told the women [newly converted] not to laleo that is, not to converse."

The law to which Paul appeals in verse 34 Bristow says is the law of love *(agape)*, and the code is the Golden Rule. The women are to be subject *(hupotasomai)* to others in this matter of being quiet, out of reverence for Christ (Eph. 5:21).

Hesuchia: A Purposeful Silence

In Jewish communities girls and women were educated only, or at least mainly, in domestic matters. This was true among the Greeks also, except for the *hetaerae* (courtesans), the companions of men. The Apostle, however, in establishing churches insisted that women be educated in the faith. Because of their lack of the discipline of study, he said they were to learn "in quietness" (1 Tim. 2:11). Bristow says the word used is a lovely word, *hesuchia* (hey-soo-KEY-ah). "It does not mean simply refraining from talking. It means restful quietness, as in meditation or study." This is the word used in Acts 21:40-22:2, when the tumultuous multitude became silent and quietly attentive to what Paul had to say in his defense, after he had signalled for silence.

The Apostle encouraged Christian women to use their gifts; but they must first quietly learn, before teaching or preaching. (Bristow, pp. 60-65, 70-77.)

The Firstborn, Levitical Priesthood

The concept of "the first into battle" may give understanding of why the firstborn male was considered given to God and needing to be redeemed, and also why the priests were men.

Women ministered at the door of the tabernacle (Ex. 3 8:8), sang in the temple choir, but did not have the fulltime temple service that men had. However, having in Scripture Miriam's song (Ex. 15:21), Hannah's (1 Sam. 2:1-10), and Mary's (Luke 1:46-55), might not some of the psalms have been written by those women temple singers (2 Chron. 35:25)?

Women are primarily nurturers of the family, although men too have this trait. But women and girls have the monthly cycle, pregnancy periods of nine months, and then nursing, weaning, and training of infants. The bonding that takes place makes it natural that the husband and father go out more into the community, into temple service, and off to war if that might be called for.

This relationship was reason to number the male population, in order to know the number of fighting men who could be called up (Num. 1:3).

The slaughter of animals and procedures of sacrifice called for male strength in the priesthood.

Now, under the New Covenant, we have the spiritual priesthood of all believers (1 Pet. 2:5, 9; Rev. 20:6).

Masculine Words for God

Dr. Gilbert Bilezikian, professor emeritus of the Wheaton College Graduate School of Theology, gives helpful comment on the male designations for God. We quote:

"The fact that God's image in human life came as male and female does not mean that God is male or female, or even both at the same time. God is a spirit; he is not bound by the physical properties that determine sexual identity .... In his transcendence God is above and beyond sexuality.

His image in humans came as male and female because both are contained within the infinitely diverse resources of his being. To say that God is either male or female is to make him in our image – in fact, in just half of the image and to confuse the Creator with the human creature.

"Most of the biblical designations for God appear in the masculine gender (he, him, his, father) because the alternative would have been offensive to the idolatry-conscious, male-dominant Hebrew culture within which revelation was given in history. For similar reasons, both male and female are designated as 'man' in the creation account, not because there were differences of rank between them but because no word exists in Hebrew for 'humans' or 'humankind.' The inclusive term 'living beings' was available, but it was unsuitable to designate humans distinctly since it was used also for animals (Gen. 2:7, 19). Their concept of 'humanity' was expressed by the term 'man' without implications of male leadership. The same holds true in our own culture [written in the USA]. The Declaration of Independence states, 'We hold these truths to be self-evident, that all men are created equal ....' Replacing 'men' by 'women' in this sentence turns it into nonsense; 'men' is used to declare both men and women as equal per creation. Note too that the significance of the Incarnation is not that the preexistent Christ was incarnated in a male, but only that in Jesus the Word became flesh." (*Christianity 101*, p.122. Grand Rapids, Michigan: Zondervan, 1993.)

1 Timothy 2:12-15
More Light on a Perplexing Text

1 and 2 Timothy and Titus, known as Paul's Pastoral Epistles, deal with false teachers whose doctrine is wreaking havoc in the early church. Paul explains to Timothy why he had been left behind in Ephesus while Paul himself goes on to Macedonia (1 Tim. 1:3-4). Timothy was to stop those who taught other doctrine, distracting God's people from the truth of the gospel. In the same way, Titus had been left to set matters straight in the churches of Crete and to appoint elders who could stop false teaching (Titus 1:9-11). All three epistles address the problem of false doctrine, those who teach it, and how to counteract it.

Women in the churches were involved in one or more heresies, as teachers and as learners. We must ask whether the Apostle wishes to stop women who teach error, or to prevent women from teaching anything at any time. Younger widows had gone astray and were going from house to house "saying what they ought not" (1 Tim. 5:13). This is the context in which Paul said women are not to teach. He asks that women first learn and come to a knowledge of the truth, as over against the women who had been misled by heretics (2 Tim. 3:6-7). Women are to learn in silence and submission, a phrase from the ancient world that implied readiness to hear the will of God and to do it. Again, we ask, may they teach the learned truth? Paul affirmed women's right to teach, in accepting Priscilla's teaching of Apollos. Other instruction that woman should teach is found in Rom. 12:7; 1 Cor. 14:26; Col. 3:16; and Titus 2:3.

Coming to 1 Tim. 2:12 we note that the text contains a rare Greek verb found only here in the N.T. and not at all in the Septuagint O.T. That word, *authentein,* has several meanings, one of which is to "have authority over" NIV, bear rule over, or tyrannize. First, we look at the rest of the passage, and will then return to the word *authentein.*

1 Tim. 2:13 says Adam was formed first and then Eve. Some take this to mean that Adam was superior to Eve. But the Bible says that God, who saw that it was not good for the man to be alone, made both male and female in his own image. The Timothy text goes on to say that Adam was not deceived, but that Eve, being totally deceived, was in the transgression. Was it better that Adam sinned knowing full well what he was doing? Romans 5:12-14 and 1 Cor. 15:21-22 both declare Adam's guilt.

Looking at an Ancient Heresy

Perplexities or seeming contradictions in the Bible call for careful study and gathering as much relevant information as possible. What kind of circumstances could Paul be addressing in this passage? These Pastoral Epistles offer several clues. Paul warns Timothy to avoid silly talk that demeans God, and oppositions of "knowledge" (*gnosis*) as falsely named (1 Tim. 6:20). There was indeed an early heresy known as Gnosticism, because its adherents maintained that they had special knowledge. Many of their characteristics are like those of the heretics in these Pastoral Epistles. They oppose what Moses taught, distort stories of the Hebrew Scriptures, and subvert the message of God's Word (2 Tim. 3:8). In Acts 20:29-30 Paul had warned the Ephesian elders that heresy would come.

Gnosticism appears to have grown out of a rebellious Judaism that repudiated the Scriptures often in shocking ways. The creation story was a particular target. In general, the Gnostic myth was as follows: Eve, rather than God, gave life to Adam. Adam, created by a third-rate deity, was deceived into thinking that eating from the tree of knowledge (*gnosis*) of good and evil would bring death. Eve brought him enlightenment by giving him the fruit. The serpent was a real friend of humanity in introducing them to true knowledge, and some actually worshipped the serpent.

If Paul is refuting such teaching, then he is saying that God made Adam, and Eve could not have given him life because she was created later. God told Adam the truth about the tree and did not deceive him. Eve was the one deceived by the serpent and was led astray. We must keep in mind that at several points in his writings Paul refutes error by setting forth the truth, without restating the problem or question that he is dealing with.

In ancient Greek literature several different but related usages appear for the verb *authentein*. The term expresses the responsibility of a person in the accomplishment of an act, originating something or being responsible for it. (The derived adjective "authentic" means original or genuine.)

Understanding something of the false doctrine that was troubling the Gentile churches, if 1 Tim. 2:13-14 is intended as refutation of a Gnostic myth, we may translate 1 Tim. 2:12 as follows: "I do not permit a woman to claim or teach that Eve was responsible for man's creation." This then becomes consistent with the rest of Scripture.

Verse 15 contains another puzzle. How can women be saved through childbearing? Some think this refers to the childbearing of *the* Christ child by the Virgin Mary. Others think it says that Godfearing women will not die in childbirth. But Eve is mentioned, not Mary; and many godly women have died in childbirth. This difficult verse appears to be a refutation of the Gnostic belief that it was a disaster for women to bring more children into the material world. Gnostics longed to be free of the physical universe and taught that women might be saved by shunning marriage and becoming as "honorary" men. But Paul wanted younger widows to marry and raise a family (1Tim. 4:3a; 5:14). He was saying that as childbearers they could be saved.

With this understanding, we see in this passage an affirmation of women and a call that they should teach only what is true and in conformity to God's Word.

An abstraction by Catherine Clarke Kroeger, scholar of languages and cultures of the Bible lands and times, from the book co-authored with husband Richard Clarke Kroeger, *I Suffer Not a Woman: Rethinking 1 Timothy 2:11-15 in Light of Ancient Evidence*. Grand Rapids, Michigan: Baker Book House, 1992.

New RSV and Inclusive Language

Our Bible could seem to have been written chiefly for men, because the words man, men, brothers, appear so often, and masculine pronouns predominate throughout. Following the entrance of sin into human life men did dominate the family and society, and God consequently imparted his word through godly men, to share his truth with the nations. Male writers used masculine words which in those days were understood to include women also, when the context called for it. We still use the words "man" and "mankind" in the same way, requiring silent translation.

Most of our readers probably use an RSV or NIV Bible. Now the New Revised Standard Version is available, having what is termed inclusive language. That is, the translators used words that include women when it is evident that the original writings meant for them to be included. Studying in depth the context, and with increasing knowledge of ancient cultures and languages, skilled translators aim at conveying *now* the meaning the words had *then*, many centuries ago.

Examples:

Adam: Hebrew "of the earth," equivalent to "human," from the Latin *humus*, which too means "earth, ground." See page 36 for use of the word "adam" in the Creation story. Dr. Bileszekian, page 76, says that no word for humans or humankind exists in Hebrew. In word-for-word translation, then, adam would have to be translated something like "earthlings." In its first appearance in Genesis, *adam* meant human or humankind. It came to mean "man" usually, and became also the personal name of Adam, after Eve was formed from him.

Greek anthropos in the N.T., translated man in the older English Bibles, is the word from which "anthropology" comes, the study of the human race. When the context shows that the word *anthropos* is not referring specifically to a male, the NRSV translators show this. Example: Romans 6:19 RSV: "I speak after the manner of men" (*anthropinos*) becomes "I speak in human terms" NRSV. Ephesians 6:6 says slaves are to obey "not in the way of eyeservice, as men-pleasers" (*anthropapeskoi*). NRSV has "not while being watched, and in order to please them" (ref. earthly masters, Eph. 6:5).

The English languages does not have a non-gender third person singular pronoun denoting either male or female as do the plural pronouns "they, them, their." So one has to say "he or she," or someone, or person, etc., or else continue the traditional use of "he, him, his" as including a woman also. There is increasing dissatisfaction with this practice, and writers and schools have been substituting the plural "they," etc.

Brothers or brethren (*adelphoi*) in Paul's greeting to congregations, in the NRSV is "brothers and sisters" with a footnote: Gk *brothers*. In both secular and NT Greek of the times the plural adelphoi could mean either males or both sexes, according to context. The similar word for sisters, *adeiphai,* made it easy.

The pronounced tendency to address men is seen in texts such as Romans 12:6 NIV: "If a man's gift is prophesying, let him use it in proportion to his faith. If it is serving, let him serve, if it is teaching, let him teach." But the Greek does not say "man" or use masculine pronouns. The NRSV says "We, who are many, are one body in Christ... We have gifts that differ according to the grace given to us: prophecy, in proportion to faith; ministry, in ministering; the teacher, in teaching, the exhorter, in exhortation."

Another example of the RSV favoring masculine terms is Acts 2:15 in which Peter indicates those who had been speaking in tongues as "these men." The text simply says "these," without *anthropoi*. Acts 1:14-15 makes it clear that the believers gathered at Pentecost included women; and 2:16-17 RSV emphasizes that all, "sons and daughters, menservants and maidservants," were filled there... and prophesied.

Genesis 2:24
A Mandate Neglected, with Tragic Consequences

Dr. Katherine Bushnell (1856-1946) a medical missionary doctor and scholar of Hebrew and Greek, through her efforts to combat enforced prostitution in America, India, and China, gained keen awareness of the oppression and exploitation of women. In the 100 Bible studies in the book that comprises the doctor's legacy, *God's Word to Women,* her treatment of Genesis 2:24 (repeated by our Lord in Matthew 19:4-5 and by the Apostle Paul in Ephesians 5:31) speaks eloquently to the scene of married life in much of India. Following the scripture, *"Therefore shall a man leave his father and his mother and cleave unto his wife."* Dr. Bushnell's first paragraph reads:

"Obedience to this fundamental marriage law of Gen. 2:24 would have saved women from ever becoming mere chattels, and thus have kept the entire race on a higher level .... The factors that would operate to relieve the oppression of Asian women would be as follows: (1) The husband, as a *bread-winner,* would have a pecuniary value in the home of his wife whereas, as it is now, the wife, as a producer of more children to be fed, is subject to abuse, more particularly when she brings forth a female child. (2) Man, not handicapped by unborn children, nurslings, or a helpless little brood, could not be reduced to slavery in an alien home, because he would forsake it and leave his helpless wife and children for those who abused him to support. But the hampering effects of motherhood and the strength of mother-love leave the mother a victim in the home of those who would enslave her. (3) Man is not so constituted that he can be robbed by force of his virtue, or his person be made a matter of trade and gain for an alien household; but these calamities are so frequently the lot of a widow left in the home of her deceased husband, that in some Asian countries, notably India, the very word 'widow' is disreputable. (4) Before gestation and parturition a mother would generally be tenderly cared for if with her own mother, under her father's roof, or nearby. But in an alien home she is often shamefully neglected at such times; and this weakens the entire race in course of time. (5) The practice of keeping the daughter at home after marriage and sending the son out of the home after marriage would put a tremendous check upon child-marriage, since parents would be in no great haste to part with the wealth-producing members of the family." (*God's Word to Women,* 1923, 390 pages, available from Christians for Biblical Equality, P.O. Box 7155, Minneapolis, MN)

In the hundreds of sermons and Bible studies heard over the years, we have never heard exposition of that thrice-repeated foundational statement. But ancient practice is evident in the marriage proposals of Issac and Jacob, and in Samson's marriage (Judges 14:1-15:2). Circumstances, of course, placed Moses in the household of his father-in-law, Jethro. Very early histories give evidence of matriarchy, echoed also in cities and towns being referred to in the feminine. We present Dr. Bushnell's insight because of the plight of India's women and girls, seen in the media and the Indian census, and known very well by India's people. Traditional practices relating to marriage are not the only debilitating factor, yet they are major.

Nationwide changes in centuries-old marriage practices may be a utopian dream. Christians can be thankful that their women-folk on the whole have better care. They can introduce their neighbors to the Bible, at this point. Parents, brothers, husbands-to-be must take to heart the message of this foundational creation statement, and share God's concern for vulnerable brides and young mothers. At the very least, a young girl should not be sent far from family and without protection, in hope of earnings.

Pastors and Bible teachers are responsible to expound Genesis 2:24, with the principles of family care and responsibilities involved. And churches that are at all able need to make a necessary part of their ministry the thoughtful help especially, but not only, for their own poor, so that girls are not endangered.

The statement of Genesis 2:24 by Father, Son, and the Apostle has been sadly neglected; and women and girls, and the nation itself, have paid a great price.